THOMAS JEFFERSON AND THE FOUNDATIONS OF AMERICAN FREEDOM

SAUL K. PADOVER

Professor, Political Science
Graduate Faculty, New School for Social Research

AN ANVIL ORIGINAL
under the general editorship of
LOUIS L. SNYDER

D. VAN NOSTRAND COMPANY, INC.
PRINCETON, NEW JERSEY
TORONTO   LONDON
NEW YORK

FOR
PEGGY

D. VAN NOSTRAND COMPANY, INC.
120 Alexander St., Princeton, New Jersey (*Principal office*); 24 West 40 St., New York, N.Y.
D. VAN NOSTRAND COMPANY (Canada), LTD.
25 Hollinger Rd., Toronto 16, Canada
D. VAN NOSTRAND COMPANY, LTD.
358, Kensington High Street, London, W.14, England

PRINTED IN THE UNITED STATES OF AMERICA

PREFACE

Thomas Jefferson came as close as any man in history to the Platonic ideal of philosopher-as-ruler. His personality was a combination of thought and action to a degree still unmatched. Jefferson's career was conspicuous both for his ideas and for his statesmanship. Few other men have left so lasting an imprint on American civilization.

James Madison, himself a statesman of broad erudition, considered Jefferson "the most learned man" ever to hold public office. The eminent Philadelphia scientist Benjamin Rush called Jefferson a citizen of the world and one who was enlightened in all the fields of science. Abraham Lincoln, nurtured on the Declaration of Independence, referred to Jefferson's principles as the "definitions and axioms of free society." Woodrow Wilson spoke of Jefferson's ideas as burning "sources of light." The late President John F. Kennedy, addressing a large group of distinguished American scholars, artists, and scientists in the White House, remarked wryly that here was the greatest collection of talent "since Jefferson dined alone" under this roof. Kennedy did not exaggerate.

Jefferson was, indeed, a scientist, scholar, jurist, philosopher, architect, inventor and, withal, a superlative political leader. One of the major founders of the American republic, he was active in public life for some four decades, roughly from 1770 to 1809. But the years of his retirement were not idle. They continued to be creative. Until his death in 1826, he devoted himself to the promotion of public education, which culminated in the creation of the University of Virginia.

Jefferson's contributions to America were numerous, varied, and enduring—notably the founding of the Demo-

cratic Party and the Louisiana Purchase—but perhaps
foremost among them was his lifelong championship of
democracy. He did more than espouse the ideal of freedom and equality; he explored its possibilities, clarified
its ramifications, and developed its principles with a full-
ness and consistency never attempted before. He left so
ineradicable a stamp on the whole range of democratic
ideas and practices that nowadays, when Americans re-
fer to democracy, they are likely to use the expression
"Jeffersonian democracy."

Here, then, is a study of Jefferson's basic thought, at
the center of which lay the idea, as well as the ideal, of
freedom.

SAUL K. PADOVER

New York City

TABLE OF CONTENTS

Part I

HISTORIC ROLE

The principles of Jefferson
are the definitions
and axioms of free society.
Abraham Lincoln, April 6, 1859

— 1 —

EARLY YEARS

Early Biography. Thomas Jefferson was born on April 13, 1743, in Shadwell, Albemarle County, Virginia, near the Blue Ridge Mountains. His father, Colonel Peter Jefferson, was a substantial citizen, a self-taught surveyor and a member of the Virginia House of Burgesses. His mother, Jane Randolph, belonged to an old Virginia family with "aristocratic" pretensions and influential connections all over the state. Peter Jefferson, a staunch Whig with the strong democratic inclinations of a self-made pioneer, had a lasting influence on his son Thomas.

Upon the death of his father, in 1757, the 14-year-old Thomas, as the eldest son among eight children, became the head of the family. The responsibility—"without a relation or friend qualified to guide me," he said—helped to mature him early. In March 1760, at the age of 17, Thomas entered William and Mary College, from which he graduated two years later. The college, despite its smallness, had resources and a few men—foremost among them Dr. William Small, a philosophical scientist, and George Wythe, an impressively learned jurist—who decisively shaped Jefferson's mind. Dr. Small, Jefferson said, "probably fixed the destinies of my life"; and Wythe became his law teacher and lifelong friend and counselor. (*See Reading No. 1.*)

William and Mary College opened up for Jefferson a whole new world of ideas, especially in the fields of science and the rational philosophy of the eighteenth-century Enlightenment. The young student read, absorbed, and often annotated virtually everything that was available in the college library, from mathematics, me-

8

chanics and music, to history, literature and philosophy. By the time he left college, at the age of 19, he was already a well-educated gentleman with a sound knowledge not only of natural science but also of the world's literature, the English common law, and languages. He had a mastery of Greek, Latin, and French, to which he later added Spanish, Italian, German, and Anglo-Saxon.

Jefferson practiced law from 1767 until 1774, when he abandoned the profession, at which he was highly successful, for private pursuits, primarily agriculture and books. His marriage to a young heiress, Martha Wayles Skelton, in 1772, added to his extensive farm holdings, so that he possessed approximately 10,000 acres. But Jefferson was not a wealthy man, and never became one. Although land-rich, he was always money-poor. His acreage, which had to support a large family and many slaves and retainers, was encumbered with debts, an economic condition that was to plague him intermittently until the end of his life.

In 1769, Jefferson became a member of the Virginia House of Burgesses, where he served for half a dozen years, until his election to the Continental Congress in 1775. This was a crucial period when American colonial opinion regarding independence from Great Britain was being crystallized. Jefferson contributed to a focusing of that opinion in his publication, *A Summary View of the Rights of British America*, which appeared in the summer of 1774. In this somewhat sharply worded pamphlet, Jefferson argued that Americans were entitled to the same natural rights as other freeborn Englishmen, and that neither King nor Parliament could have any arbitrary power over them. (*See Reading No. 2.*)

A Summary View, which was widely read, may be considered Jefferson's historic debut. His name, which henceforth was to grow steadily in fame, was now known enough to attract attention. In London, the British Government placed him on a list of its enemies. As Jefferson put it, *A Summary View* "procured me the honor of having my name inserted in a long list of proscriptions enrolled in a bill of attainder." In Philadelphia, in 1776, he procured a greater honor, that of drafting the Declaration of Independence. In the Declaration, echoes of which are found in *A Summary View,* Jefferson immortalized himself with his proclamation of the rights and liberties of man, written so eloquently that the words and phrases have reverberated through the years. (*See Readings Nos. 3; 4.*)

Service During the American Revolution. During the Revolutionary War, Jefferson was active in the affairs of his native state, being elected to the legislature in 1776 and to the governorship in 1779. As a legislator, he served on a committee, consisting of the eminent jurists Edmund Pendleton and George Wythe, to codify Virginia's antiquated laws. A master legal draftsman, Jefferson contributed most of the work. He was particularly proud of having drafted the laws to abolish entail; to repeal primogeniture; to separate Church and State (*see Reading No. 5*); and to establish a system of general education. The first two acts were designed to do away with the remnants of feudalism; the second two were meant to further the spirit of freedom. In his *Autobiography,* Jefferson said of them: "I considered four of these bills, passed or reported, as forming a system by which every fibre would be eradicated of ancient or future aristocracy; and a foundation laid for a government truly republican."

Similarly, he made important liberalizing contributions when he served in the Continental Congress in 1783-1784. A member of nearly every major committee, he drafted 31 papers ranging from domestic finance to foreign treaties. Two of these papers were especially noteworthy for their influence. His *Notes on the Establishment of a Money Unit* (April 1784) later led to the adoption of the dollar as the United States money standard. His *Report on Government for Western Territory* (*see Reading No. 6*) became the basis for the 1787 Northwest Ordinance, which included the vital provisions of self-government and the abolition of slavery in the future states of the Middle West.

Diplomatic Service in Europe. For about six years, from 1784 to 1789, Jefferson was American Minister in Paris. Europe became for him the last stage in his intellectual development, widening his horizons and deepening his convictions. He traveled in France, Holland,

Germany, England, Italy, and always with a purpose: to learn. Notebook in hand, his eyes sharpened by science, his mind boundlessly inquisitive, he carefully observed everything—the shape of an arch, the structure of a bridge, the song of a nightingale, the value of the olive, the importance of rice, the potential of the (newly invented) steam engine, the layout of cities, the plans of gardens, the design of wheel barrows, the breeding of pigs, the behavior of kings. Every observation he made would, he was sure, be somehow useful to America.

In Paris, Jefferson associated with some of the foremost literary, philosophical, and political personalities. Among the latter were those who made the French Revolution. Jefferson quietly cautioned them against extreme radicalism, advising them to accept democratic reforms by the monarchy. His counsel went unheeded. Extremist action by the French Revolutionists was to result, as Jefferson suspected it would, in a generation of violence and dictatorship. (*See Reading No. 7.*)

The intellectual atmosphere during Jefferson's stay in Paris was heady with exciting social and political ideas. Hopes for human improvement and universal freedom moved men's souls. They left a permanent stamp on Jefferson's ideals of scientific rationalism as a means to cure the ills of mankind, and political democracy as a guarantee of human happiness. These were, Jefferson held, the highest goals of humanity and, if revolutionary action was called for to achieve them, he did not flinch from it. Thus, in his letters from Paris, he defended Shays' Rebellion in Massachusetts (1768-1787), which frightened conservatives in America.

Defends Revolution. Jefferson's defense of Shays' uprising formed a kind of democratic theory of revolution. It consisted of three main points. The first was the assertion, also found in the Declaration of Independence, that the people, being the ultimate source of all government, had a right to correct their just grievances by force if their rulers ignored their demands. The second was the assumption that the rebellion, a rarity in America, was a temporary aberration correctible by proper information, education, and the "good sense of the people." (*See Reading No. 8A, D.*) The third was the principle that the *spirit* of rebellion was a necessary safeguard of freedom, to be kept alive rather than discouraged. Rebels of the Massachusetts type should not be punished by means of any tyrannical institutions, for this would be "setting up a kite to keep the henyard in order." Without occasional rebellion, the rulers would become lethargic and indifferent to the needs of the people. "The tree of liberty," Jefferson wrote, "must be refreshed from time to time with the blood of patriots & tyrants. It is its natural manure." (*See Reading No. 8B, C.*)

In the same sense, Jefferson justified the French Revolution. Even after the revolutionists indulged in excesses, which shocked him personally, he continued to defend the Revolution itself on higher grounds, namely, as a major historic event that promised to lead to the establishment of republicanism and freedom in Europe and ultimately perhaps in the rest of the world. Jefferson, viewing the French Revolution as a great battle in the liberation of humanity, assumed that a certain cost in human lives was to be expected, as in any war. Hence even the Reign of Terror and Jacobin intolerance did not alienate his sympathies towards the basic aims of the French Revolution. (*See Reading No. 9.*)

Washington's Secretary of State. Upon his return to the United States, at the end of 1789, Jefferson became Secretary of State in George Washington's Cabinet. He resigned four years later, largely because he found himself increasingly out of sympathy with the President's conservative policies. The spokesman of these policies was Alexander Hamilton, the brilliant and ambitious Secretary of the Treasury, with whom Jefferson was in almost constant conflict. The clash between them spilled over into the press, wherein Hamilton flatly accused Jefferson of having opposed the Constitution and of being hostile to the policies, especially the financial ones, of the government. Jefferson, who, in his letters from Paris, had actually supported the Constitution but urged the need for a Bill of Rights (*see Reading No. 10*), in turn charged Hamilton with intolerable meddling and with pursuing a deliberate policy of corrupting the legislature. (*See Reading No. 11.*)

Conflict with Hamilton. Jefferson's conflict with Hamilton, fascinating both as drama and as history, was personal only to a limited extent. The two men were, to be sure, sharply contrasting personalities—Jefferson tall, calm and poised; Hamilton slight, restless and insecure—and obviously not sympathetic to each other. But the conflict transcended the personal. Theirs was a clash over principles and ideas that each considered fundamental and, therefore, irreconcilable. Their conflicting philosophies, shared by large or influential numbers of Americans, involved momentous public issues that had an effect on the course of the country's development. Indeed, their antipodal positions were reflected and crystallized in the formation of America's first competing political parties: Democrats (then known as Republicans), founded by Jefferson and Madison in the 1790's, and Federalists.

Apart from disagreement over foreign policy—Jefferson being pro-French and Hamilton pro-British—there were two basic points of difference between them. One was political and the other economic, but in reality the two meshed to form an integrated public philosophy. To use the traditional labels, it may be said that Jefferson was a democrat in politics and an agrarian in economics, while Hamilton was an aristocrat in politics and a capitalist in economics.

Jefferson believed in rule by the majority, preferably by land-owning farmers. Hamilton was convinced that the best government was that of an elite, made up of the "rich and the well born." Jefferson was shocked when he heard Hamilton, who never made any secret of his antidemocratic bias, say that corruption and force were necessary to govern men. In his diary (*The Anas*, 1791), Jefferson reports Hamilton as saying that the British political system, precisely because it was run on corruption—that is, by an hereditary or financial aristocracy motivated by special economic privileges—was the "most perfect government which ever existed."

Jefferson's Agrarianism. Jefferson felt that any privileged class, especially such an urban commercial one as was developing in America largely under the stimulus of Hamilton's economic policies, was a menace to democracy and freedom. He saw no virtue in commercial pursuits or in city life. Contrary to Hamilton, he based his hopes for a libertarian republic on farmers and not on merchants or urban dwellers. Jefferson's agrarian and anti-urban philosophy was influenced by the eighteenth-century Physiocratic doctrines, which were reinforced by his observations of the slums of Europe, particularly those of Paris and London.

Jefferson explained his agrarianism on two general grounds, one of morality and the other of existing American realities.

Morally, he was convinced that the man who farms and, in particular, owns his own land is a better person in every way than he who is propertyless or pitifully dependent upon another for his daily bread. As he saw it, those who were engaged in trade were corrupted by money, and those who worked for others were degraded by the lack of it. The majority of laborers, underpaid and ignorant, lacked the moral qualities for successful self-government. They were, as the British example showed, hardly better off than Negro slaves in America. (*See Reading No. 12.*)

In an agrarian society, on the other hand, agricultural pursuits created ideal people for the maintenance of a self-governing republic. Agriculture imbued man with a sense of independence, dignity, freedom, "virtue," and love of country. "The cultivators of the earth," Jefferson repeated frequently, "are the most virtuous citizens, and possess most of the *amor patriae.*" Farmers, he said, were "God's chosen people," and the more there were of them the healthier the republic was likely to be. (*See Reading No. 13.*)

The American realities gave force to Jefferson's view of the desirability of agrarianism. The great majority of the people in his day were rural and made their living in agriculture. Jefferson was sure that they were happy, certainly happier than the people of England or France, and virtuous. There were no slums in America, and no permanent body of hopeless poor, as in Europe. (*See Reading No. 12.*) "If ever the morals of a people could be made the basis of their government," he told John Adams in 1796, "it is our case."

Jefferson hoped that this unique American situation, which he considered ideal, would continue. For one thing, there was ample land: "We have now lands enough," he told John Jay, "to employ an infinite number of people in their cultivation." For another, the agrarian economy had certain inestimable advantages, among them self-sufficiency and the priceless possibility of avoiding war. Unlike an industrial or mercantile economy, agrarianism had no need for foreign trade and hence was not vulnerable to attacks on the high seas, a recurring cause of international conflict. To maintain peace and the national well-being, Jefferson thought that the wisest policy would be to continue to maximize agriculture, at least so long as land was available, and to minimize commerce. He believed that the needed manufactured articles had best be imported from Europe in return for American raw materials. (*See Reading No. 14.*)

In the end, this aspect of his agrarian philosophy was nullified by world conditions. The global conflict between the British and French empires, which lasted for a quarter of a century, all but destroyed American shipping on the seas—and with it Jefferson's dream of an agricultural, nonmanufacturing republic. The Anglo-French wars, which virtually closed the oceans to neutrals, made Jefferson realize the danger and folly of depending upon the outside for necessary products. "Experience has taught me," he wrote a third of a century after he had first formulated his proagrarian thesis in the *Notes on Virginia,* "that manufactures are now as necessary to our independence as to our comfort." His final conclusion, representing a complete reversal of position, would surely have pleased Hamilton: "We must now place the manufacturer by the side of the agriculturist." (*See Reading No. 15.*)

His Vice-Presidency. Upon retirement as the Secretary of State, in December 1793, Jefferson spent three years in his beloved Monticello, improving his farms and land, which had been neglected during his long periods of public service. In the Presidential election of 1796, he was a candidate so reluctant to run that he did not do any campaigning. Even so, he received 68 electoral votes to John Adams' 71, which, under the law as it then existed, made Jefferson Vice-President. It was an innocuous post, described by John Adams, when *he* was Vice-President under George Washington: "My country has in its wisdom contrived for me the most insignificant office that ever the invention of man contrived or his imagination conceived."

Jefferson, who shared Adams' view on the subject, entered into the Vice-Presidency lukewarmly, but consoled himself with the idea that the "tranquil" office, as he called it, would at least keep him out of the violent political strife that he had found so distasteful when he served in Washington's Cabinet. The Vice-Presidency, he told a friend, would "give me philosophical evenings in the winter, and rural days in summer."

It did not altogether turn out that way. The Vice-Presidential chair may have been a tranquil one, but the country was not. The nation was split over relations with France, and party feelings, always violent, ran higher than ever. After the so-called "X.Y.Z." Affair" of 1797—an emotional outburst resulting from the news that French Foreign Minister Talleyrand's agents had asked American diplomats in Paris for a bribe of $240,-000—the publicly incensed Federalists moved to take action not only against French agents and agitators in America but also against native American critics of the Adams Administration. They passed the Alien and Sedition Acts, which were to have a profound effect on Jefferson's political position and career.

Alien and Sedition Acts. The Alien Acts (June and July 1798) consisted of three provisions. One required that the period of naturalization be extended from 5 to 14 years, a measure designed to keep immigrants with their prodemocratic sympathies out of political life. (This was repealed by the Jeffersonians in 1802.) Another authorized the President to deport all aliens deemed dangerous to the country; this was aimed particularly against the anti-British Irish. The third empowered the President to jail or expel citizens of an enemy nation, in this instance mainly French, in time of war. Jefferson, in a letter to Madison, called this antialien legislation a "most detestable thing."

Far more serious, in the eyes of Jefferson and his democratic followers, was the Sedition Act. This "gag-law," as Jefferson referred to it, was intended to crush all native American opposition. The Act made it a crime, punishable by a fine up to $2,000 and imprisonment up to two years, to criticize the Administration directly or indirectly. Under this Act the Federal government prosecuted 25 persons and convicted 10 of these people, among them those who had merely printed (in one instance an announcement of a lottery to pay the fines) unfavorable reflections on the Federalists. All of the victims, including those in jail awaiting trial, were prominent Jeffersonian-Republican editors and leaders.

The shocked Jefferson reacted strongly in his dual capacity as a political leader and as a believer in democracy. The Federalists, who hated and dreaded his party for its alleged radicalism, were clearly determined to destroy it by jailing its leaders and gagging its editors. They hoped thereby, Jefferson was sure, to intimidate the common people and thus cripple his Republican party.

As a democrat, Jefferson viewed the Alien and Sedition Acts as a massive assault on his political philosophy. He was convinced that this legislation was but a first move—"an experiment" in public opinion, he called it—in a calculated Federalist program to establish aristocratic government in the United States. "If this goes down," he wrote privately, "we shall immediately see attempted another act of Congress, declaring that the President shall continue in office during life, reserving to another occasion the transfer of the succession to his heirs, and the establishment of the Senate for life."

The Kentucky and Virginia Resolutions. As Vice-President, Jefferson could not move openly against the Administration of which he was officially a member. But convinced that freedom and the republic were imperiled, he had to act. This he did indirectly. In consultation with like-minded friends, he decided that the first move should come through the State governments, the "bastions" of freedom. The result was the famous "Kentucky and Virginia Resolutions," passed by those State legislatures in November and December 1798, respectively. Jefferson was the secret author of the Kentucky Resolutions and Madison of those of Virginia.

In the Kentucky Resolutions, a landmark in United States Federalism, Jefferson fully developed the compact theory of the Constitution and, within this framework, argued that the Alien and Sedition Acts were unconstitutional. He made the following constitutional points: (a) the Federal Constitution, a compact among the States, had created a strictly limited national government; (b) it was granted certain definite, enumerated powers, and no more; (c) the "residuary mass of rights," including freedom of religion, speech and press, were retained by the States; (d) the States were the sole judges of their rights and of infractions upon them; (e) the Alien and Sedition Acts dealt with freedom, a subject that, under the Constitution, was reserved to the States. Therefore, Jefferson concluded, the Alien and Sedition legislation, not being within the jurisdiction of the national government, was "altogether void, and of no force." (*See Reading No. 16.*)

The Kentucky and Virginia Resolutions must be viewed from two angles, the theoretical and the particular. As theory, they reflected a significant aspect of the Jeffersonian philosophy of government, namely the desirability of decentralized power. Jefferson feared strong government as a matter of principle. "I am not," he told Madison, "a friend to a very energetic government. It is always oppressive." But he dreaded it particularly in the United States, which was geographically too big to make centralized power compatible either with good government or with freedom. In a country the size of the United States, and at a time of primitive transportation and communication facilities, public servants were so far removed from the watchful eyes of their constituents that detection of wrongdoing was all but impossible. A concentration of political power in geographically gigantic America, Jefferson feared, would make it "the most corrupt government on earth."

To avoid such "corruption, plunder and waste," therefore, it was necessary to divide and localize governmental functions as widely as possible. (*See Reading No. 17.*) Implicitly, this theory, of course, underlies the Federal Constitution. Jefferson always believed that so long as power was scattered among the far-flung states, it was practically impossible for it to be usurped, as was the case in Europe, by any one person or group for purposes of establishing a centralized tyranny. Hence he called the state governments "the true barriers of our liberty." (*See Reading No. 17A.*) Such, in short, was Jefferson's rationale, a fundamentally democratic one, of the principle of States rights.

More specifically, the Kentucky and Virginia Resolutions were designed to undermine the constitutional ground on which the Federalists stood. Jefferson hoped that the Resolutions would penetrate the country (or be adopted by other state legislatures, a hope which did not materialize), help crystallize public opinion by educating the people as to the basic constitutional points at issue, and supply his followers with an arsenal of arguments against Federal usurpation. But he also knew that more than mere legal propositions would be needed to save the republic from the peril of oligarchical rule. Freedom could be secured only by winning political power. And so he began quietly to mobilize the forces of republicanism, which he sensed and, as it turned out, correctly so, to be a majority of the American people, for the Presidential election battle of 1800.

Presidential Candidate and Platform. This time, he was no longer a reluctant candidate. The struggle, he knew, would be bitter and rough. It would also be decisive, since it would determine once and for all the course that young America was to take—aristocratic class rule, or democratic self-government. Now Jefferson, although he never ceased to yearn for the serenity and beauty of his beloved home in Virginia, unhesitatingly undertook to lead in a cause he considered the greatest and noblest in the world—the cause of freedom and popular government. If victorious, he would have to forego gratifying personal pursuits—family life, gardening, reading, scientific inquiries—and give himself to the nation for many more years.

In the absence of party organizations or written platforms in the modern sense, Jefferson operated through personal contacts and communication with key leaders. Insofar as he and his Republican-Democratic party had a specific program, it can be found in his letters to important figures. One of these communications, to the Massachusetts Republican-Democratic leader Elbridge Gerry (later Governor and U. S. Vice-President), may be considered as a party platform. It contained what Jefferson called "a profession of my political faith." Through this and similar communications, which were of course expected to be made public, Jefferson wanted his followers to know what, as he said, "I am for" and "I am not for."

He was *for:*

The preservation of the Federal Constitution as it was originally intended; States rights; a "frugal and simple" government; a militia and a navy for defense only; free commerce with all nations; freedom of religion; freedom of the press; encouragement of the sciences.

He was *not for:*

Hereditary rule and a "monarchising" Federal government; an all-powerful national administration; an increasing public debt; a standing army and an aggressive navy; international entanglements; religious and intellectual intolerance. (*See Reading No. 18.*)

— 2 —

THE PRESIDENCY

The Presidential Campaign. The Presidential campaign of 1800 was fiercely fought in an atmosphere of political passions that Jefferson described as "awful." The Federalists accused him of virtually every crime in the Decalogue, including thievery, immorality and, most damning of all, godlessness. The clergy, convinced that under the Jeffersonians their influence would decline, were particularly virulent in their animosity. Their fulminations led Jefferson to make a memorable remark. Referring (in a letter to Dr. Benjamin Rush: September 23, 1800) to the clergy's belief that he was opposed to clerical domination, he wrote: "And they believe rightly; for *I have sworn upon the altar of God, eternal hostility against every form of tyranny over the mind of man*." The words italicized here are inscribed, by order of Franklin D. Roosevelt,* inside the Jefferson Monument in Washington, D. C.

The election resulted in a Republican victory. The ticket headed by Jefferson and Aaron Burr carried the Southern States plus New York, for a total of 146 electoral votes. Two Southern States (Maryland and North Carolina) and Pennsylvania split their vote. The Federalists under John Adams and Charles C. Pinckney won the New England States and New Jersey which, together with the split vote, gave them an insufficient total of 129. Their defeat turned out to be irremediable. The Federalist became, in Jefferson's words, "all head and no body," and never recovered as a political party.

---

* At the suggestion of the late Secretary of Interior Harold L. Ickes and Saul K. Padover, the author of this book, who selected the quotation.

The Complicated Election. For Jefferson and his party, the victory was complicated by a technicality. The Constitution at that time did not call for a specific designation of Presidential and Vice-Presidential candidates. Article II, Sec. 1, merely provided that the Electors should vote "for two persons" and that the one who received the highest number of votes "shall be the President" (this was changed by the 12th Amendment in 1804). In case of a tie, the House of Representatives was to "choose the President." Jefferson and Burr had received an identical number of electoral votes—73 each —and so the election was thrown into the House of Representatives. Even though it was clear that the electorate had meant Jefferson, and not Burr, to be President, nevertheless party passions, aggravated by some chicanery, resulted in a prolonged deadlock. It was not broken until February 17, 1801, when Jefferson (helped by the influence of Alexander Hamilton, who considered Burr a greater evil) was elected on the 36th ballot.

Jefferson viewed his election not as a personal triumph but as a victory of principle. He considered it a "pacific revolution, as real as that of 1776." For one thing, the nation had unmistakably repudiated the Federalists and their openly antidemocratic policies and principles. For another, the election vindicated Jefferson's political philosophy and his faith in the ultimate good sense of the people. It showed, he said, that no matter how disappointing popular aberration may be, it was bound to be temporary, and therefore the "good citizen must never despair of the commonwealth."

The Significance of the Election. The election, as Jefferson saw it, taught another lesson. It disproved a widely held theory, propagated by Montesquieu and others, that democratic (or republican) government could exist and be preserved only in small countries. For America, such a theory was pernicious. The election now also proved it to be untrue. If United States territory, Jefferson pointed out, had been even one-third the size it was, he and his Republicans would have lost. But the very bigness of the country saved the democracy; it gave time and opportunity to those who were temporarily misled to recover their senses and rejoin those who had remained democratically staunch. As Jefferson put it: "While frenzy & delusion like an epidemic, gained certain parts, the residue remained sound and untouched, and held on till their brethren could recover from the temporary delusion."

The "revolution" of 1800, Jefferson was convinced, transcended in its significance the borders of the United States. It had world importance. In a universe ruled mainly by monarchs, aristocrats and autocrats, a triumph of democracy and republicanism in one country was bound to serve as a heartening example to men who struggled for freedom everywhere. America was the "world's best hope," Jefferson said, and as such it was under moral "obligation" to be humanity's beacon of liberty. (*See Reading No. 19.*) Incidentally, this was a view shared and expressed by America's foremost leaders before and after Jefferson, from George Washington's First Inaugural ("the preservation of the sacred fire of liberty, and the destiny of the republican model of government, are justly considered as deeply, perhaps as finally staked, on the experiment intrusted to the hands of the American people") to Franklin D. Roosevelt's Four Freedoms.*

One of Jefferson's first, and in some ways most important, moves as President was to bring harmony to a nation torn by unprecedented party strife. (*See Reading No. 20.*) He realized, as did his disciple Abraham Lincoln some six decades later, that national hatred, whether engendered by politics or religion, was an enemy of freedom and order. Without concord and affection, Jefferson said, "liberty and even life itself are but dreary things." He was, therefore, determined to assuage political wounds, to conciliate his opponents by moderation, and to assure them of his respect for honest differences of opinion. "The greatest good we can do our country," he wrote to the distinguished jurist John Dickinson in the Summer of 1801, "is to heal its party divisions and make them one people."

The First Inaugural Address. It was in this spirit of harmony and mollification that he wrote and delivered

* See S. K. Padover, *The Genius of America* (1960), pp. 12-14.

his First Inaugural Address in Washington, on March 4, 1801. The eloquent Address, a classic worthy to be ranked with the Declaration of Independence, is best understood, in terms of Jefferson's own approach, as operating on two levels. One was as a vehicle for public education and enlightenment; the other, as a formulation of the democratic philosophy.

It should never be forgotten—and Jefferson, for one, never permitted himself to forget—that he lived in an age when the ideal of popular government held a precarious position in men's minds. It had few supporters of any eminence. It was actively opposed, and often ridiculed, by the powerful, the learned, and the influential practically everywhere, including the United States. (Hamilton, for example, considered the mass of the people "vicious," and John Adams regarded them as unable to "judge, act, think, or will.") Despite all that, the democratic ideal was making headway in Jefferson's day. Nevertheless, it was so relatively novel and untried on any large scale that its meaning and practical potentialities were not yet clearly understood even by those who gave it ardent support.

Jefferson, therefore, conceived it his duty to act in a dual capacity, that of a champion of the forces of freedom and of an explicator of its philosophy. He was, on the one hand, a practical political leader—a tough-minded and in the long run supremely successful organizer of America's democratic movement; and, on the other hand, an indefatigable teacher of the principles and practices of self-government. Wherever and whenever possible, he tried to act and write in such a way as to impress the people—in those days as yet largely without elementary education—with some object lesson in liberty and self-government. As he put it in a letter of instructions to his Attorney-General Levi Lincoln, he wanted his public utterances to be occasions for "sowing useful truths and principles among the people, which might germinate and become rooted among their political tenets."

The First Inaugural Address was, for Jefferson, a splendid occasion to spell out to the nation the fundamental ideas in which he believed. It consisted of two main parts, a general and a particular. The first portion explained the meaning of republican government and the fortunate position of the United States, emphasizing freedom of opinion, rule by the majority, and respect for the minority. (*See Reading No. 21A.*) These principles, Jefferson said, "should be the creed of our political faith, the text of civic instruction."

The second part, in effect an elaboration of his letter to Elbridge Gerry (*see Reading No. 18*), enumerated the points of policy by which he expected his Administration to be guided. Here he listed, among other things, peace and neutrality, reliance on militia, civilian supremacy over the military, payment of the national debt, frugality, encouragement of agriculture and commerce "as its handmaid." (*See Reading No. 21B.*) The whole Address was studded with memorable phrases: "Every difference of opinion is not a difference of principle." "Error of opinion may be tolerated where reason is left free to combat it." "We are all Republicans, we are all Federalists." "Honest friendship with all nations, entangling alliances with none."

The First Administration. Jefferson's Presidency was, beyond doubt, a turning point in history. It reversed the trend, set in motion by the ardently class-conscious and often brilliantly articulate Federalists, towards oligarchy, aristocratic pomp, and suppression of opinion. Jefferson and the Republicans, assisted by such gifted men as James Madison (Secretary of State) and Albert Gallatin (Secretary of the Treasury), deliberately launched the United States on the opposite road—that leading to genuine popular government, marked by democratic simplicity, secured by a widening suffrage, stimulated by confidence in the common people, and invigorated by an atmosphere of freedom. From that day to this, the United States has never seriously swerved from the democratic path marked out by Jefferson. If anything, it has steadily enlarged it. As Lincoln said, Jefferson's principles have remained "the definitions and axioms of free society."

The American people obviously approved the Jefferson program, which a young New England orator named Daniel Webster described as something made up of "fantastic dreams" invented by "opinionated visionaries."

Despite continued Federalist hostility, often wildly intemperate in tone (*see Reading No. 22*), Jefferson was overwhelmingly re-elected in 1804. He swept the country with 162 electoral votes, as against 14 for his Federalist opponent Charles C. Pinckney, carrying every State in the Union, except Connecticut and Delaware. He even won the 19 electoral votes of Massachusetts with 29,310 popular votes against Pinckney's 25,777.

The President's Policy of Simplicity. Contrary to the dire predictions and gloomy expectations of the Federalists, Jefferson's Administration was not marked by radicalism. It neither undermined property, nor subverted religion, nor corrupted morals, nor destroyed the Constitution, nor encouraged mob rule. But it *was* different from those of his predecessors in some significant respects. One difference was in the President's general attitude or, one might say, in his psychological stance; another, in certain of his policies.

On a personal level, the President's behavior involved a special kind of subtlety. Historically, he knew, chiefs of state and rulers had always used impressive titles and ostentatious pomp to keep their subjects in a condition of abjectness and insidious intimidation. Jefferson decided to abolish such age-old techniques of domination and to institute, instead, a deliberate policy of republicanization —through simplicity. He would tolerate no artificial distinctions—he even objected to such customary titles as "Honorable" and "Excellency"—and no barriers between leader and citizen. In every possible way he would act so as to set the people an example of republican unostentatiousness. This public policy fitted his private personality. A man of exquisite courtesy and impeccable manners (*see Reading No. 23*), he was as devoid of affectation as of social prejudice. "If it be possible to be . . . conscious of anything," he said, "I am conscious of feeling no difference between writing to the highest and lowest being on earth." The record bears out this self-estimate.

Reversing the ceremonial proceedings of George Washington and John Adams, Jefferson had himself inaugurated President with calculated republican unostentatiousness. There were no parades or coaches or uniforms. On March 4, 1801, accompanied by a group of friends and citizens,

without guards or servants, he went on foot from his un-
pretentious boardinghouse to the unfinished Capitol to be
sworn in. The third President of the United States took
the oath of office dressed in "plain cloth."

This deliberate plainness continued to characterize the
next eight years of the Jefferson Administration. Feeling
that to address Congress in person, as his predecessors
had done, was reminiscent of the monarchistic "speech
from the throne," he inaugurated the practice (discon-
tinued by Woodrow Wilson 112 years later) of sending
written messages by hand. He discouraged celebrations of
his birthday. In the President's house, John Adams' beloved levees—European royalistic morning receptions
attended by the socially ambitious—were pointedly done
away with by Jefferson. He did it by indirection. When
the Washington ladies showed up for the expected levee,
the new President, suave and gracious as usual, received
them smilingly—in spurred boots and still dusty from
his morning ride. The discomfited ladies got the point,
and the levee was buried forever.

At social gatherings, the President made it a point of
ignoring differences in rank or position. At dinners,
everybody was seated in what he called *pêle-mêle* fashion,
ladies in general preceding gentlemen to the table. Even
foreign diplomats, always acutely sensitive to protocol,
were treated in this studied republican manner. When
the ranking British Minister expressed outrage at what he
considered an insult to His Majesty, and protested the
"incivility" to London, Jefferson blandly explained that
Washington, D.C., was not the Court of St. James but
the capital of a republic: "The principle of society as
well as of government, with us, is the equality of the
individuals composing it." He added that here no man
would come to dinner if he were to be "marked with
inferiority" to any other.

His overriding concern was to establish what he called
"the chastity" of republican government and "to fence
out" every practice that might tend to weaken it. One of
the things that he was adamant about fencing out was
political gifts. He knew that the practice of giving and
taking largesse, for purposes of influencing political decisions, was both ancient and universal. In his opinion, it

tended to corrupt the officeholder and to perpetuate injustice. Concerned, therefore, with the purity of republicanism, he made it "an inviolable rule" never to accept any gift of pecuniary value. This, he said, was to him a sacred law, necessary as a salutary example for the country and the tranquillity of his own mind.

Freedom of Opinion—An "Experiment." In another area of public behavior, that of freedom of opinion, Jefferson was also determined to set an example that would serve as a guide for the future. This was both more painful and more difficult than the practice of republican integrity, because it involved deep human emotions. The President, it should be remembered, was under constant personal attack. His party was viciously libeled. His ideas were vilified. Tradition, law, and normal human feelings, all were on the side of prosecution for libel. Both as a man and as a leader, Jefferson was put to the severest test and, indeed, the temptation was ever present. But, despite some recent accusations of Jeffersonian violation of the democratic philosophy, made academically outside the context of the desperate contemporary battle for the establishment of the republican ideal,* Jefferson, nevertheless, did firmly live up to the practice of freedom, including the freedom to criticize him and the government. Referring to bitterly unfair newspaper attacks, he said: "I shall protect them in the right of lying and calumniating." (*See Reading No. 24.*)

Jefferson's position in defense of the right to express opinions, regardless of their veracity, reflected both a personal attitude and a philosophical conviction. In per-

* See L. W. Levy, *Jefferson & Civil Liberties: The Darker Side* (1963). The instances cited by Professor Levy, including cases from Jefferson's wartime governorship of Virginia, are true individually. They show that Jefferson was not primarily an abstract philosopher of freedom, but a soldier in the battle for its maintenance. In his total commitment to the republican-democratic idea, he did not, as a practical political leader, hesitate to use expedient means when the preservation of the cause of Freedom called for it. Those, in any case, were rare enough. To dwell on this as the "darker side" is to distort the whole spirit of the man and the meaning of the history of his time. It is like painting a man's warts rather than his face.

sonal relations he never indulged in controversy, but always listened politely. He used to illustrate the "inutility" of conversational argument by an anecdote of two men who began to discuss a subject and ended with each converting the other. "I tolerate with the utmost latitude," Jefferson told Abigail Adams in 1804, "the right of others to differ from me in opinion without imputing to them criminality." When someone disagreed with him, he quietly changed the subject: "I say to myself, he has a right to his opinion, as I to mine; why should I question it?" (*See Reading No. 25.*) He hoped that reason and experience would in time correct the other man's error.

The decision not to prosecute the press for libel was an agonizing one. Jefferson and his party were constantly exposed to "thousands of calumnies" (*see Reading No. 26B*) of a nature that no "stomach could bear." (*See Reading No. 26C.*) Grievously tempted to strike back legally, he toyed with the notion of an admonitory prosecution of the worst offenders in State courts. (*See Reading No. 26D.*) In the end, however, he concluded that the long-range interests of freedom necessitated a policy of no interference with the press, no matter how venal and vicious it might be. This, Jefferson reiterated privately and stated publicly in his Second Inaugural Address, was America's novel "experiment" in self-government (*See Reading No. 26A.*)

Jefferson's reasoning in support of this policy was within a consistent democratic framework. It may be summarized in capsule form as follows: Free government requires that the citizen have "all the avenues to truth" open to him. The most effective channel found so far was the press. (*See Reading No. 27.*) At its best, that is, when it was guided by the truth, the press was "a noble institution, equally the friend of science & of civil liberty." (*See Reading No. 26B.*) When the press lied and indulged in irresponsible smears, it should not be shut up or destroyed as an institution, for such a policy would seal off a potentially useful avenue to public knowledge and enlightenment. Instead of undermining the freedom of the press, it was wiser to trust the good sense of the people to serve as the ultimate corrective to falsehood. In this way "the inestimable liberty of the press" could be preserved. (*See Reading No. 28.*)

This self-emendatory aspect of Jefferson's "experiment" in freedom was rooted in the gigantic assumption, which, indeed, underlies democracy in general, that man was a rational being, guided by reason and not by emotion. As such, the average citizen was thought to be capable, at least in the long run, of separating the true from the false. He might be temporarily misled by plausible lies and inflamed by base emotions, but in the end rationality would assert itself. On this premise, Jefferson believed that man could govern or be governed "by reason & truth," rather than by dogma and violence. (*See Reading No. 27.*)

In the realm of politics, three events in the Jefferson Presidency are of particular interest. One was the acquisition of the Louisiana Territory; another, the Embargo; the third, reduction of the national debt. Each of these illuminates a facet of Jefferson's career and illustrates his pragmatic character.

The Louisiana Purchase. The Louisiana Purchase revolved around the problem of New Orleans, the gateway to the Mississippi, which was the lifeline of the American West. Under the rule of weak Spain, Americans enjoyed free navigation of the river, and the "right of deposit" of their goods in New Orleans. Late in 1801, the disturbing news reached Jefferson that the aggressive Napoleon had obtained Louisiana from Spain. The President, sensitive to the needs of an expanding West as well as to the threat to the national security, was convinced that a strong foreign power in control of New Orleans was the "natural and habitual enemy" of the United States.

Jefferson was determined to go to any lengths to meet the threat. He even considered reversing the hitherto hostile relations with Great Britain, a country whose government he detested. Should French troops set foot in Louisiana, he said grimly, it would be necessary to "marry ourselves to the British fleet and nation." In the meantime he instructed the American diplomat, Robert R. Livingston (joined in Paris by James Monroe), to negotiate for the purchase of the "island" of New Orleans. Fortunately, Napoleon, preparing for another round in his global war with Great Britain, needed money and suddenly offered to sell the whole Louisiana Territory, and not just New Orleans. The Americans, caught by surprise, nevertheless bought the territory. On May 2, 1803, they signed a treaty, acquiring, for approximately $15,-000,000, a region as big as Western Europe. Out of this one million square miles of Louisiana Territory were subsequently to be carved not only the States of Louisiana and Arkansas but also the great American West—Colorado, North Dakota, South Dakota, Iowa, Kansas, Minnesota, Missouri, Montana, Nebraska, Oklahoma, and Wyoming.

This was not only the greatest real estate bargain in history, but also, on a political level, Jefferson's crowning achievement. The Louisiana Purchase presented the President with a problem of conscience in regard to the Constitution. He knew, beyond any doubt, that the Constitution neither empowered such acquisition nor provided for its incorporation into the Union. The Federal compact was confined to the original States of the American Revolution, and not to foreign territory. By conviction, Jefferson was a "strict constructionist" in regard to the Constitution, believing that any "loose" interpretation of it opened up dangerous possibilities for abuse of power. And the whole Louisiana action, he admitted frankly in a private letter to a friend, was "beyond the Constitution."

He was willing to violate his own principles and become, for the moment, a "loose constructionist" because of what he believed to be the greater good, of interest to "every man in the nation." This national good included an elimination of foreign powers from the borders of America, an avoidance of war with France, an opportunity to secure the peaceful development of the expanding country and, not least, the doubling of the size of the United States as an "island of freedom" and happiness for ever larger numbers of people. All this was of such incalculable (Jefferson used the word "inappreciable") importance that he overcame his Constitutional scruples and had the treaty hurried through the Senate for ratification (October 17, 1803) before Napoleon could change his mind or domestic "malcontents" could raise a hue and cry against it. (*See Reading No. 29.*) But Jefferson was never quite happy about his questionable role in dealing, or rather not dealing, with the constitutional issue involved in the Louisiana Purchase.

The Embargo and Non-Importation Policies. Jefferson's foreign policy, as embodied in the Embargo (December 1807) and Non-Importation (April 1808) Acts, constituted a noteworthy experiment in international relations. In the global Anglo-French conflict, neutral American shipping was caught in the cleft stick of the British blockade of French-dominated Europe and the French counterblockade of Britain. Neither the whale nor the mammoth, as Jefferson called the British and French Empires, had the smallest regard for American rights on the seas. Napoleon, for one, contemptuously referred to the American flag as "only a piece of striped bunting."

Jefferson, an ardent pacifist who detested British imperialism as vehemently as he abhorred Napoleonic militarism, was determined not to get involved in what he called the bloody "Arena of gladiators." For one thing, the United States was neither strong nor rich enough to fight a foreign war. For another, there was nothing to choose between the belligerents: both were hostile to America. And yet the continuing injury to American interests could not be ignored. Jefferson, therefore, decided upon an economic course of action. In the "present paroxysm of the insanity of Europe," he concluded that the wisest policy was "to break off all intercourse" with that Continent. This meant closing the American ports to foreign trade.

The Embargo policy not only failed to achieve its objectives abroad but also backfired at home. Jefferson had miscalculated the whole situation. In regard to Europe, he had overestimated the European, especially the British, dependence upon American food and raw materials. The economic deprivation, it turned out, was not serious enough to make the British change their policy towards the United States. It was, in fact, the Americans rather than the Europeans, who suffered the consequences of the Embargo. It led to many business bankruptcies, unemployment in the commercial States, flagrant smuggling, and a sharp drop in the President's popularity. As British Foreign Minister George Canning remarked sar donically, the Embargo was a "measure of inconvenient restriction upon the American people."

Under powerful and highly vocal public pressure, Jefferson was forced to rescind his nonintercourse policy before he left office. But he remained convinced that the Embargo was fundamentally a wise course, an experiment in the politics of peace that was not given a fair trial. In his defense, it should be pointed out that early nineteenth-century economics, particularly foreign trade and its consequences, was still a comparatively primitive science. In the absence of a body of accurate and disciplined data to serve in the making of decisions, the statesmen in Jefferson's day had to be guided mainly by personal theories. These were not necessarily wrong.

Financial Policy—Elimination of Debt. More satisfactory to Jefferson, both psychologically and politically, was his debt policy. On a personal level, he regarded debt as a constant "torment," a "thraldom of mind." A man who owed money, he felt, was never really free from worry and pressure. Jefferson repeatedly preached the rule of not purchasing anything unless one had ready cash. "The maxim of buying nothing but what we have money in our pockets to pay for," he told a relative, "lays, of all others, the broadest foundation for happiness." To his chagrin, in his private life he was rarely able to live up to his own laudatory maxim.

But he was more successful with the national debt. The principle, ascribed to the Hamiltonians, that "a public debt is a public blessing," Jefferson repudiated as pernicious. It was, he was sure, a public curse. It mortgaged the future and burdened the present. It was a standing enemy of liberty and happiness.

In this area, Jefferson's position was partly that of an agrarian and partly that of a humanist. Basically, his reasoning was that a public debt involved growing interest payments, that is, the enrichment of nonproductive bankers at the expense of producers; interest payments necessitated ever higher taxation, that is, the imposition of financial loads on the poor, who could least afford it; and such an increasing tax burden ultimately resulted in the virtual enslavement of the great majority of the people. (*See Reading No. 30.*) This was the case in England, which Jefferson once referred to as "a nation of pikes and gudgeons, the latter bred merely as food for the former," and other European aristocracies and monarchies. Nothing, Jefferson believed, was so "corruptive of the government and so demoralizing of the nation as a public debt."

Consistent with this economic philosophy, he made the retirement of the national debt the prime concern of his Administration. He considered this part of his program, as he told his Secretary of the Treasury Gallatin, "vital to the destinies of our government." (*See Reading No. 30A.*) Devotedly assisted by the able Gallatin, Jefferson followed three lines of economic policy: No borrowing; extinguishment of the funded debt by systematic payments of principal and interest; reduction of expenditures. Furthermore, internal taxes, such as the unpopular levy on whisky, were abolished. The whole program was surprisingly successful.

Before Jefferson left office, his Administration had paid off $33,580,000 of the debt (out of a total indebtedness of some $80,000,000), which was, the President said, "within the limits of the law and our contracts." In his last Annual Message (November 8, 1808), he was able to announce with quiet satisfaction a treasury surplus of about $2,000,000. He suggested that Congress consider using the money for the "improvement of roads, canals, rivers, education, and other great foundations of prosperity and union."

Refusal to Accept a Third Term. On March 4, 1809, Jefferson retired from the Presidency. Despite "general solicitations," including the requests of five state legislatures, that he run again, he refused to consider a third term. His decision was in part personal but mainly a matter of principle. The Presidency was undoubtedly a burden. In a letter to the Philadelphia physician Caspar Wistar, Jefferson spoke yearningly of a lifelong desire to be a scientist instead of his present occupation in the "dry & dreary waste of politics." Some of the Presidential functions, such as removals of people from office, were "horrid drudgery" and made him feel, he said, like "a public executioner." In the middle of his second term he confided to his friend Lafayette: "I am panting for retirement."

Fundamentally, however, Jefferson's refusal to run for
third term was rooted in his general philosophy of free
overnment. When, in Paris, he had first read the Con-
itution, he had been troubled by the fact that it put no
mit on the number of times a President could be re-
lected. Here, he feared, was a loophole through which
ereditary rule might slip. The lesson of history, he said,
owed that legally unlimited tenures easily "slide into
heritances." (*See Reading No. 31B.*) Originally, there-
ore, he favored a single Presidential term of seven years
nd permanent "ineligibility afterwards." (*See Reading
o. 31A.*)

George Washington and his two terms, terminated by
oluntary retirement, made Jefferson change his mind in
vor of the first President's precedent. The third Presi-
ent came to realize that it was wiser and safer to have
vo four-year terms—the first to be a "period of proba-
on," he said—and then retire voluntarily. He hoped that
ucceeding Presidents would follow this historic precedent
 that in time it would become a "salutary" principle
yally supported by the people. Jefferson, therefore, de-
berately followed the example of Washington.

— 3 —

LAST YEARS

Retirement from the Presidency. In the Winter of 1809, when Jefferson left the Presidency, he had been in the public service for nearly 40 years. Returning home to Monticello and receiving a warm welcome from his fellow Virginians—in sharp contrast to the harsh criticism of his Embargo policies in the North—the 66-year-old statesman-philosopher made a characteristically moving reply:

"Of you, then, my neighbors, I may ask, in the face of the world, 'Whose ox have I taken, or whom have I defrauded? Whom have I oppressed, or of whose hand have I received a bribe to blind mine eyes therewith?' "

He had the satisfaction of knowing that freedom was safe in the hands of his dominant Republican-Democratic party and that he had given the best that was in him to the creation of a libertarian and humane government in the United States. The importance of this transcended America, which Jefferson referred to as "this solitary republic" and "the sole depository of the sacred fire of freedom and self-government" in the world. In his farewell address to the citizens of Washington, D. C., he expressed the hope that this sacred flame would be "lighted up in other regions of the earth."

Jefferson's contribution to a democratic America was momentous. He had reversed the possibility—perhaps the certainty—of class government and had firmly launched the United States on its historic democratic career. He lived long enough to see his two most devoted friends and closest collaborators, James Madison and James Monroe, occupy the Presidency for the next 16 years and follow the path he had charted. Both of these Presidents in succession continued to consult their "tutelary genius"

36

(as Madison called him) on major political questions, such as the Monroe Doctrine. After 24 unbroken years of what is known as the "Jeffersonian system," the American republic was never to swerve from its democratic course.

For the last 17 years of his life, Jefferson lived withdrawn from public service, but he was not really "retired." He was as busy as ever. As his grandson remarked of him, the only thing with which he was niggardly was time. Rising regularly at dawn, Jefferson was active until late at night. The days were devoted to the business of making a living, primarily farming his extensive but run-down acreage. The nights were given to reading, particularly philosophy and the classics in the original, and to writing, mainly correspondence.

Flooded by Letters. A torrent of letters, from strangers and friends, among them leading scholars, scientists, and political figures, kept pouring steadily into the home of the famous "Sage of Monticello." In one year (1820) Jefferson counted no less than 1,267 letters. The aging statesman, troubled by the pressing necessity of time-devouring replies, groaned under what he called a "persecution of letters." He met this "epistolary *corvée*" by answering as many as he could—some through a polygraph which he invented. His letters have become not only a treasury of Americana but, what is more important, a delightful source of Jeffersonian ideas.*

His Educational Plans. Jefferson's final contribution to his country was not in the field of politics, but of education. After surveying educational systems and ideas in

---

* During his lifetime, Jefferson wrote about 18,000 letters and received approximately 25,000. Most of them have been preserved, and about four volumes a year are now being published by the Princeton University Press, under the editorship of Julian P. Boyd and associates. The first volume of *The Papers of Thomas Jefferson* came out in 1950. The total is expected to be 52 volumes, making it "the richest treasure-house of historical information ever left by a single man."

For collections of some of Jefferson's most interesting letters, see S. K. Padover, *A Jefferson Profile* (1956); and L. J. Cappon, *The Adams-Jefferson Letters: The Complete Correspondence Between Thomas Jefferson and Abigail and John Adams* (2 vols., 1959).

other lands, he carefully worked out a plan for his native State, hoping that it would also serve as a model for others. He proposed a three-part public-school system: elementary schools to teach the three R's and geography; high schools to instruct in foreign languages and to prepare students for the professions; and, finally, the state university. The latter was to be the culmination of the whole system. This new plan was an elaboration of his Bill for the Diffusion of Knowledge that he had drafted as a young man in 1778. (*See Chapter 8.*)

His Creation of the University of Virginia. Jefferson spent eight years, from 1817 to 1825, creating the University of Virginia. This, he told a European friend, was "the last of my mortal cares, and the last service I can render my country." In every way, it was a stunning achievement, not the least so for being, in its entirety, the single-handed creation of a man in his seventies and eighties.

At Charlottesville, on 250 acres of land within sight of his own Monticello, Jefferson laid out the campus of the first important tax-supported university in the United States. He personally drafted the architectural designs. He prepared the landscaping. He procured the artisans and sculptors. He supervised the bricklayers and the carpenters. He cajoled the reluctant state legislators to allocate ever larger sums. (The final cost of construction was $300,000, a big amount for those days.)

In addition to the physical details, Jefferson also planned the whole curriculum, established the academic organization, and used his wide contacts for the recruitment of professors, "of the first grade of science in their respective lines," mainly from Europe. The goal of the university was to train a "multitude of fine young men" in the "useful" branches of science, including desirable (republican) political science, and to elevate their minds and characters so that they would worthily serve the self-governing republic.

The University of Virginia, with its "chaste and classical" architecture, dominated by the beautiful Jefferson-designed rotunda, opened its doors in 1825. It was the crowning act of Jefferson's life. One year later, on July 4, 1826, he died at the age of 83. His death marked the passing of a giant from this earth.

— 4 —

HUMAN NATURE AND MORALITY

Jefferson's Epitaph. Before his death, Jefferson left precise instructions on what to inscribe on his tombstone. Visitors to Monticello can still see the words engraved on the obelisk over his grave:

> "Here was Buried
> Thomas Jefferson
> Author of the Declaration of American Independence
> Of the Statute of Virginia for Religious Freedom
> & Father of the University of Virginia."

This was all—"& not a word more," he wrote—that he wanted to be remembered for, and it may, therefore, be considered as a final estimate of what he thought significant. Jefferson's self-appraisal may well serve as a guide to the analysis of his basic ideas.

Each of the three items listed on his tombstone highlights essential facets of the Jeffersonian creed. The Declaration of Independence, in its brevity (about 1,300 words) and stylistic beauty,* is the quintessence of the democratic philosophy and has been repeatedly proclaimed as such, not only in the United States but also abroad. Virginia's *Statute for Religious Freedom* (*see Reading No. 5*) served as a model for others and was a heartfelt expression of what Jefferson considered to be of supreme importance for liberty in general. The founding of the University of Virginia was a practical manifestation of the significance of science and learning in a demo-

* It can be read like poetry. See S. K. Padover, "Jefferson Prose Poem: The Declaration of Independence," in *American Mercury*, February 1942.

cratic republic. All together, these three aspects—democratic belief, religious freedom, and education—explain the Jeffersonian political philosophy.

Let us begin with general beliefs and assumptions.

His Theory of Human Nature. A proper understanding of Jefferson's political creed requires a knowledge of his psychological beliefs. His theories of government were built on his conception of the character of man. It is, of course, true that all political theories must make certain explicit or implicit assumptions about human nature. Authoritarian government, whether aristocratic or monarchical, rested on the ultimate belief that man was unworthy or incompetent, or both. Popular government, whether a limited republic or a democracy, had, on the contrary, to assume that human beings, or at least a substantial portion of them, were potentially good and capable of using power responsibly, if not always necessarily with prudence.

Jefferson, unlike such eminent contemporaries as John Adams and Alexander Hamilton, accepted the logic of his democratic position, namely, that man was innately virtuous, rather than incorrigibly vicious. Without such a belief, indeed, he could not have espoused the cause of self-government, or perhaps any other type of decent government. For the acceptance of the notion of human depravity involved a possibly insoluble contradiction. Clearly, it made no sense to assume the possibility of successful government by human beings who were inherently wicked and evil. This is what Jefferson meant when, referring in his First Inaugural Address to those who claimed that man could not be relied on to rule himself, he asked with rhetorical irony: "Can he, then, be trusted with the government of others? Or have we found angels in the forms of kings to govern him?"

Jefferson knew that much of the weight of European political tradition and scholarship was against his faith in human goodness. With rare exceptions, notably John Locke, authoritative writers had long ago taken a dour view of human nature. The erudite Jefferson was innately familiar with established political theory, including the writings of such towering authorities as Niccolo Machiavelli and Thomas Hobbes, whose pessimism about the character of man was widely shared in Europe. In his classic work, *The Prince,* Machiavelli built his political theory on human cowardice and greed. "For it may be said of men in general," he wrote (Ch. 17), "that they are ungrateful, voluble, dissemblers, anxious to avoid danger, and covetous of gain; as long as you benefit them they are entirely yours."

Hobbes' *Leviathan,* no less influential than *The Prince,* took an equally gloomy view of human nature. Man, according to Hobbes, was an egoistic creature dominated by his instincts, among them vanity, lust, and avarice and living in "continuall feare" of his fellows, because the latter were motivated by the same ugly instincts. These passions, he wrote, produce in "all mankind a perpetual and restlesse desire for power after power, that ceaseth only in Death." The consequence of such unceasing lust is "Warre, of every man, against every man." Only powerful government can restrain these ugly propensities.

Jefferson, knowing these theories, felt that they may have been applicable to Europe, but hardly to America. They explained, he was sure, Europe's political "organization of kings, hereditary nobles, and priests." The European denial of human goodness left no alternative but force as an instrument of rule. Europe's rulers, Jefferson said, used the theories of human beastliness to justify their exploitation of the people, to deprive them of their political rights, and "to keep them down by hard labor, poverty and ignorance." (*See Reading No. 32.*)

As Jefferson saw it, American realities did not lend support to the pessimistic theories of human nature. There were no Borgia princes in Virginia. In the part of the country with which Jefferson was familiar, men were not engaged in unending war with each other. If they engaged in struggle, it was with nature rather than with one another. If they lusted, they were likely to do so for whisky or a wench, but not for domination over their fellow citizens. Among Jefferson's neighbors, farmers all, he could detect no evidence that would confirm Hobbes' description of the human being as *homo homini lupus*-man is a wolf to man. Nor did his own observations corroborate the belief of such famous European writers as La Rochefoucauld and Montaigne that "fourteen out fteen men are rogues." The frontiersmen whom Jefferson new were more honest than deceitful, more cooperative han wolfish.

The psychological theory which Jefferson found sympathetic was that of John Locke, the philosopher whom e perhaps most admired. In his *Essay Concerning Human Understanding* (1690), Locke took the empirical position, en quite revolutionary, that human behavior, as well as nowledge, derived from experience. Man's character was ot predetermined biologically but was shaped after birth, y the life he led and by the milieu in which he lived. n another essay, *Of the Conduct of the Understanding*, Locke argued that skills, even those that depended on the aind, were not "natural" but "the product of exercise." efferson accepted this view of the environmentalists who, a his day, had a saying that "a button maker becomes a utton and a buckle maker a buckle in the course of his fe." Man, in other words, is not born a maker of buttons r buckles; he becomes so through his environment.

The logic of this position led to the conclusion that a ood environment could create virtuous people; a bad ne could do the reverse. To produce desirable human eings for the good society, it was, therefore, necessary to uild a proper milieu—which, above all, included the ght kind of government—to make it possible for men flourish and to pursue the great goals of life, liberty, nd happiness. To Jefferson, an instinctive empiricist and xperimenter, the environmentalist psychological theory as the ultimate in common sense.

A further logical step within this framework was the cceptance of the principle that the people were the urce of all just power in society. This, Jefferson said, as the "true bottom" of the whole philosophy of self-overnment. (*See Reading No. 33.*) He regarded the octrine of such importance that, in mentioning David ume's famous criticism of it as noble but "specious," : permitted himself a rare outburst of anger: "And here else will this degenerate son of science, this traitor his fellow men, find the origin of just powers, if not the majority of the society? Will it be in the minority? r in an individual of that minority?"

Jefferson constructed his whole political philosophy on

trust in the character of man, both as an individual an as a member of society. Here, indeed, lies one of Jeffe son's major contributions to the politics of the moder world. He felt that not only was all power ultimate "bottomed" on the people, but, what was equally im portant, they were its only safe depository. Nobody els could or should be trusted with political power. This in volved the vital belief, from which Jefferson never flinche that the people were capable of governing themselv and that, therefore, they should exercise government functions on as wide a scale as was consistent with th order and security of the society. So far as he was co cerned, there could be no other limits to the people participation in political affairs. It was, after all, *the* government.

Jefferson saw no merit in the ancient argument of th antidemocrats, among them leading and respected Amer can contemporaries, that the people in general had neith the ability nor the character to exercise power responsibl He insisted that they possessed both. If their abili was insufficient, that is, if they were not enlightene enough, the obvious remedy, he said, was not to depri them of their rights and opportunities, but to infor them through education. (*See Chapter 8.*)

Reason and Morality. As for character, Jefferso took the classic position, shared by such esteemed seve teenth-century writers as Sir Algernon Sidney and Joh Locke, that man was a "rational animal." Nature, sa Jefferson, endowed man not only with reason but al with natural rights and an "innate sense of justice" ar morality. He assumed that there could be no free gover ment without moral principles and without virtuous pe ple. A classic example of immorality and its deterio effects was the Roman Republic, which, Jefferson point out, collapsed because the nation was "steeped in corru tion, vice and venality." The Roman people were t "demoralized and depraved" to be capable of exercising wholesome control over their Republic or to retain the liberties. (*See Reading No. 34.*) They, therefore, fell pr to dictatorship and Caesarism.

What, then, were moral principles and where did m

rality come from? Jefferson believed that man was a moral creature and that his principles were rooted in a "moral instinct" with which he was born. Moral principles were "innate elements of the human constitution." They included a sense of justice, deference for the law, respect for the rights of others, generosity, and compassion. All of this could be summarized in one word—goodness. "The greatest honor of a man," Jefferson, when President, told the chief of the Shawnee Indians, "is in doing good to his fellow men." In their aggregate, these moral tenets constituted the "essence of a republic." (*See Reading No. 35.*)

The "Moral Instinct." The moral faculty, Jefferson said, did not derive from organized religion or from the "love of God," because there was ample evidence of the existence of morality among atheists. Nor was morality altogether a matter of egoism or self-interest, as the French philosopher Claude Adrien Helvétius argued in his book, *De L'Esprit* (1758). Jefferson, citing Helvétius, agreed with him that good acts give man pleasure, but he asked why they did. His answer was that the human being gets enjoyment out of being benevolent to his fellow creatures because it was a "natural" feeling. "Nature," Jefferson wrote, "hath implanted in our breasts a love of others, a sense of duty to them, a moral instinct, in short, which prompts us irresistibly to feel and to succor their distress."

Since the "moral instinct" was not designated by any physical earmark in the human body, how could one identify it? Jefferson admitted that morality was relative: actions considered virtuous in one country were deemed vicious in another. But they were identifiable by *utility,* which nature had made the standard of morality and virtue. Different cultures had different sets of customs and goals, but each was, nevertheless, guided by its own morality, as determined by social usefulness. No matter how varied and diverse human behavior might be, the moral sense was always there.

The existence of innate "moral instinct" had to be assumed rationally, Jefferson argued, because without it society would be an impossibility. An individual when he is alone can indulge himself in every possible way; he has no responsibility to or for anything but his own appetites. Hence he neither has nor needs to have morality, since the latter by definition involves relations with other people. But social organization, or civilization, was a fact of history; consequently, one had to assume that there was *something* inside the human being that made it possible and that did, indeed, impel men to live together in society. That *something* had to be inherent in man—in other words, an "instinct" with which he was born. "The Creator," said Jefferson, "would indeed have been a bungling artist" if he had intended man for a social animal without implanting in him "social dispositions."

Virtually all human beings possessed this moral instinct, or "internal monitor," as Jefferson sometimes called it. The rare few who were born without it, as some were also born without limbs or senses, were more degraded than those who suffered from the most hideous bodily deformities. Such were criminals and amoral political adventurers (Bonaparte, for example, whom Jefferson detested). In self-protection, society must attempt to correct its moral deficiency through education. But in the great majority, the moral instinct remained as the "brightest gem" in the human character. (*See Reading No. 36.*)

Man, in sum, was a moral and rational creature, able to differentiate between right and wrong, between justice and injustice. His moral instinct guided him in making decisions as to what was good or bad for him and for society. Hence there could be no question about his ability, even apart from his natural right, to govern himself, even if, for practical reasons, he had to do so indirectly. If, Jefferson said, the average citizen did not have the training to be an executive, he did have the intelligence to "name the person" who did. If he was not sufficiently skilled to pass legislation, he was qualified to "choose the legislators." If he was not educated in the law to be a judge, he was "very capable of judging questions of fact" as a juror. (*See Reading No. 37.*)

Jefferson summarized his democratic faith in a famous sentence in a letter to his friend Pierre Samuel Dupont de Nemours. Referring to both himself and his friend as men who cherished the people as their children, he wrote: "But you love them as infants whom you are afraid to trust without nurses; and I as adults whom I freely leave to self-government." (*See Reading No. 35.*)

— 5 —

LIBERTY AND NATURAL RIGHTS

Natural ("Unalienable") Rights. In the Declaration of Independence, Jefferson wrote that the rights to life, liberty, and the pursuit of happiness were "inherent and unalienable." Although Congress struck out "inherent and," and substituted the word "certain," nevertheless "inherent" was precisely what Jefferson meant. To him, it was "self-evident" truth, which lay at the base of his whole political thought, that man was born with certain "natural rights."

The natural rights doctrine was both an ethical norm and a political guide. It was, as Abraham Lincoln once explained, a standard of orientation for free men. The theory can be traced back to the Middle Ages, but for Jefferson it was made cogent by English and French writers of the seventeenth and eighteenth centuries. Notable among them were John Locke and Jean Jacques Burlamaqui (1694-1748), a professor of law at Geneva, Switzerland.

Jefferson was, of course, intimately familiar with these, as well as other political philosophers, including Jean Jacques Rousseau (whom he rarely quoted and for whose writings he seems to have had scant sympathy). In his *Treatises Concerning Government* (1690), Locke had developed the classic theory of natural rights, speaking of man as being "naturally free" and as being born with a title to "an uncontrolled enjoyment of all the rights and privileges of the law of nature." Jefferson considered Locke's book "perfect as far as it goes."

Burlamaqui's *Principes du Droit Naturel,* published in English as *The Principles of Natural and Politic Law* (1748), was used as a textbook at Cambridge and Oxford, as well as at William and Mary (from 1779 to 1840), and was widely printed and read in America. It was frequently quoted by leaders of the American Revolution. Jefferson knew Burlamaqui at first hand and probably also discussed his theories with George Wythe, an admirer of the Swiss author.* The word "happiness," instead of Locke's "property," in the Declaration of Independence, may be traced to Burlamaqui. According to him, man was "made for happiness," and the pursuit of it was the "key . . of the human system." †

Jefferson used the concept of natural rights to explain and to defend a whole range of political notions, actions, and institutions. Subsumed under it was freedom, with emphasis on individual freedom. This was the pivot around which everything else revolved.

Man, said Jefferson, had a natural right to life, because he is born free, and "freedom is the gift of nature," which nobody, neither a government nor a person, can take from him. (*See Reading No. 38.*) Man had a natural right to think freely and to publish his thoughts by speaking or writing. Hence no government had a right to censor newspapers or books. If, Jefferson said, a particular book is "false in its facts, disprove them; if false in its reasoning, refute it. But, for God's sake, let us freely hear both sides." (*See Reading No. 39.*) Man had a natural right to free commerce and the pursuit of his personal calling. He had a natural right to associate freely with his fellow citizens, whether for public or private purposes. (*See Reading No. 40.*) Above all, he had a natural right to self-government. This right, coming from the "hand of nature," belongs to "every body of men on earth." (*See Reading No. 41.*)

The Natural Right to Self-Government. Self-government was the core of man's rights. Its prime purpose was

---

* For Burlamaqui's influence in America, see R. F. Harvey, *Burlamaqui: A Liberal Tradition in American Constitutionalism* (1937).
† For an extended discussion of the meaning of happiness, especially in connection with Jefferson, see U. M. von Eckardt, *The Pursuit of Happiness in the Democratic Creed* (1959).

to secure and protect all other natural rights of the citizens. This view of government involved two important consequences. One was that, being utilitarian, it was necessarily subject to constant change to meet the flux of events. The other consequence was that self-government must be limited in its power. Otherwise it would end up, as had virtually all governments in history, as a monster devouring the natural rights of the people.

Self-government meant a republic. Jefferson realized that the word was loosely used. People, he remarked, were saying that a republic "may mean anything or nothing." Examples of the vagueness of the term, he said, were the "self-styled" republics of Holland, Switzerland, Genoa, Venice, and Poland. In Jefferson's view, these were hardly republics, because their governments were either hereditary, or self-chosen, or serving for life.

What, then, was a republic? There were, Jefferson pointed out, certain yardsticks with which to measure it. Three main ingredients made up a republic. First, was election by the people; secondly, fixed (preferably short) terms of office; thirdly, majority rule. All together, they added up to the fundamental principle of all republics—control over the government by the people.

By definition, republicanism ranged all the way from "pure" to "representative," the former being direct and the latter indirect rule. If citizens acted directly, that is, conducted their affairs in a body, they lived in a pure republic. This, Jefferson thought, was the ideal state, but obviously not "practicable beyond the extent of a New England township." The size of America made it necessary to have the next best thing to a pure republic—namely, a representative one. As a general measuring rod, Jefferson suggested, governments should be viewed as being "more or less republican as they have more or less of the element of popular election and control" in their systems. (*See Reading No. 42.*)

The Function of the Constitution. Underpinning the American republic was the written Constitution. Jefferson regarded it as a purely practical political instrument designed to achieve two main purposes. One of its functions was to serve as a check on power, which, he said, always has a tendency to "degenerate into abuse." The Constitution did so in two ways. It provided for a system of government with a wide distribution of national and state powers. It also supplied a text for those who were on guard against violation of liberty, and thus it helped both to prevent and to correct abuse. (*See Reading No. 43.*) The other primary function of the Constitution was normative. It served as a general guide to political behavior. It furnished the people with standards and principles of their political creed.

But this did not mean that the Constitution was sacrosanct or immune from alteration, even radical alteration. Jefferson objected to the idea of viewing any constitution with "sanctimonious reverence," as something "too sacred to be touched." The Constitution was the creation of the people; and the government under it was only their servant. To serve the people properly, the Constitution must always adjust itself to changing times and circumstances. Jefferson even went so far as to suggest—without actually advocating—that the Constitution be thoroughly revised by each new generation, say, every 19 or 20 years, to keep up with the times. "Laws and institutions," he wrote, "must go hand in hand with the progress of the human mind." (*See Reading No. 44.*)

But change, too, had certain impassable limits. Constitutional revisions or legal alterations were defensible only within the total framework of freedom, and never against it. Under no circumstances must changes be made or legislation enacted at the expense of the institutional systems that were set up to maintain what Jefferson called "our dearest rights." Even the legislature, the ultimate expression of the people's power, must not overstep the line. Legislators, Jefferson said, must be "apprized of the rightful limits of their power." These are strictly defined by our natural rights, which the legislature may only declare and enforce, and never take from us.

Opposition to Judicial Review. This belief in the need for limiting power explains why Jefferson vehemently opposed the principle—and, of course, the practice—of judicial review, under which judges could declare an act, or part of an act, of Congress unconstitutional.

The precedent for judicial review, established by his kinsman and political enemy, Chief Justice John Marshall, in *Marbury v. Madison* (1803), Jefferson angrily rejected as "gratuitous" and indefensible. He considered it dangerous to liberty on three grounds. It was a usurpation, by the Federal judiciary, of power not granted in the Constitution. It was a disruption of the delicate system of checks and balances provided for in the Constitution. It was undemocratic, in that it was an assertion of power by judges serving for life, "unelected by, and independent of, the nation." (*See Reading No. 46.*) Judicial review, in brief, was fundamentally inimical to the philosophy of freedom and to the structure of self-government. It was a meddling with the people's natural right to legislate for themselves. To Justice Marshall's argument that, under a written Constitution, there must be a general arbiter somewhere, Jefferson's reply was: "True, there must be; but . . . the ultimate arbiter is the people of the Union," assembled by their representatives in convention, at the call of Congress or of two-thirds of the States.

To conclude: Jefferson believed that liberty could be maintained and natural rights secured only through a republican government—the only one which was not "eternally at open or secret war with the rights of mankind." Carefully hedged by institutional contrivances and Constitutional safeguards, such a government would produce "the greatest sum of happiness" for its citizens.

In this, man was no exception. Not everybody was equally talented or developed. Jefferson assumed the existence of wide differences in ability and character among human beings. Some men were endowed with special qualities, and they, Jefferson believed, formed a "natural aristocracy." The natural aristocrats were such, not because they inherited privilege or position, but because they were born with "special virtue and talents," which Jefferson considered nature's "most precious gift" to society. The main function of the natural aristocrats —selected through impartial examinations and educated at public expense—was to provide wisdom and leadership for the mass of the people, who were less wise and less gifted. (*See Chapter 8.*) Jefferson thought that the best form of government was the one led by such a natural aristocracy. (*See Reading No. 47.*)

Equality as a Political Concept. His concept of equality was, therefore, neither biological nor psychological. It was political. It meant that men were born with the right—the natural right—to enjoy the same political privileges ("liberty," "life," the "pursuit of happiness") as their neighbors. It meant an affirmation of the equal rights of every citizen in the political sphere, regardless of his talents or income. It meant the equal right to vote, to participate in governmental affairs, to acquire and hold property, and to claim equal justice under the law. It meant a rejection of the claim to special privilege or consideration by the rich and the well-born. It meant a complete repudiation of the principles and practices, then widely prevalent in Europe, of hereditary governance. To Jefferson, the principle of equal rights was the "fundamental" and "immovable basis" of republicanism in general, and of the American governments, state and national, in particular. It was, in brief, the exact opposite of the traditional rule by rank and birth or, what he called, "tinsel-aristocracy."

It was in this spirit that Jefferson protested, especially in letters to George Washington, the formation of the Society of the Cincinnati. This was an organization of disbanded officers of the Continental Army, and Jefferson, abhorring any political distinction "by birth or badge," dreaded it as a potential hereditary aristocracy—a fear sufficiently justified by the history of the origins of Europe's nobility. He considered the Society of the Cincinnati "dishonorable and destructive to our governments." (*See Reading No. 48A.*) The American governments, he reminded George Washington, the head of the Cincinnati, were built on the natural equality of man and a repudiation of "every pre-eminence but that annexed to legal office." (*See Reading No. 48B.*)

Equality Only for Whites? The question has been frequently raised whether Jefferson's idea of equality applied only to white men. When he wrote that "all men" were created equal and could claim the enjoyment of their natural rights on a basis of equality, did he mean to include persons of different color or race? How did his advocacy of equality as a universal principle accord with the institution of slavery, the denial of rights to Negroes, and the treatment of American Indians?

The answers to these questions can be neither simple nor absolutely clear. They have to be sought in contemporary perspective, on the basis of a realization—indeed, a Jeffersonian realization—that times and circumstances change radically. The eighteenth century is not the middle twentieth, and many of the emphases of the Age of Reason are not the same as those of the Age of the Atom.

In Jefferson's time, and of course long before that, political and social thought concerned itself primarily with Western man. Theories were built on, and references cited from, the experiences of Europe, including Graeco-Roman antiquity. Except for the areas and experiences mentioned in the Bible, other cultures were mostly unknown or not considered worth stressing. The modern sciences of man, notably anthropology and sociology, were nonexistent; others, particularly psychology and its sister disciplines, were as yet in embryo. The focus of social thinking was, therefore, on European man, about whom materials, both for speculation and for proof, were abundantly available in historical and literary sources. Hence when Jefferson, or for that matter, Locke, spoke of "all men," the implicit assumption was "European men." The tacit exclusion of others was not a matter of race prejudice but of habitual focus.

The America of Jefferson's day was overwhelmingly a white man's country. Most of the inhabitants were West Europeans, primarily of British stock. There were only two minority groups, Negroes and Indians. The Negroes were, with a handful of exceptions, slaves. The Indians were more or less self-sufficient "nations," and were, indeed, treated as such—including in warfare and treaty relations—by the American governments. The slaves were not in a position to claim rights; the Red men did not care to do so. In that sense, therefore, both Negroes and Indians were outside the American political community.

Equality and Negroes. This did not mean that the Negroes and Indians were ignored or rejected. Actually, these two minority groups, each in a different way, presented a continuous challenge to white Americans. Jefferson, both as a Southern slaveowner and as a statesman, evinced a constant concern with, and interest in, Negroes and Indians. There was, indeed, no possibility of escaping the reality of their existence in America.

In regard to Negroes, it is well to view Jefferson's position from two angles. One, their character and intelligence; the other, the institution of slavery.

Jefferson had, of course, ample opportunity to study Negroes at first hand. There was little else to guide him. Like most of his contemporaries, he knew little about their African origins. He could only study them as they were in America, under the unfavorable conditions of slavery. "To our reproach it must be said," he wrote in his *Notes on Virginia* (1782), where he first developed his opinions of Negroes, as well as of Indians, "that though for a century and a half we have had under our eyes the races of black and of red men, they have never yet been viewed by us as subjects of natural history." He, therefore, worked out his own natural history.

His personal observations of Negroes led him to certain conclusions, which he frankly admitted were tentative. Negroes, to begin with, were obviously different from Europeans. The most striking difference was color. Jefferson thought that nature might well have intended the Negroes' skin to be a manifestation of physiological, and hence probably emotional, differences from Europeans. In making his comparisons of them with whites,

Jefferson conjectured, subject to further proof or disproof, that Negroes were capable of the highest integrity, kindliness, and loyalty; that in music they were superior to Europeans; that in memory they were their equals; but that in reason they were inferior. "Nature," he wrote, "has been less bountiful to them in the endowments of the head," but had done them justice in those of the heart. (*See Reading No. 49.*) He expressed his opinion of the intellectual inferiority of Negroes, he said, with great hesitation.

His hesitation was justified. Some 20 years after he spoke his doubts about Negro intelligence, he received Benjamin Banneker's *Almanac and Ephemeris* (1791), which shook whatever measure of certainty he may have had about the mental inferiority of black men. For Banneker was a Maryland Negro freeman and a self-taught mathematician and astronomer.* Jefferson was so impressed that he not only helped Banneker obtain a position as assistant in the surveying of the District of Columbia, but he also sent a copy of the *Almanac* to the Marquis de Condorcet, the secretary of the distinguished Academy of Sciences at Paris, as evidence that Negroes were capable of high intellectual endeavor. To both Banneker and Condorcet, Jefferson expressed the opinion that it was possible that the reason why Negroes had hitherto shown no creative talents was, not their innate inferiority, but their "degraded condition"—that is, slavery—in America.

This environmentalist view, incidentally, was then beginning to make its way in the United States. In 1789, Samuel Stanhope Smith, Jefferson's fellow member of the American Philosophical Society at Philadelphia, published a pioneering study, *An Essay on the Causes of the Variety of Complexion and Figure in the Human Species,* in which he stated: "It is well known that the Africans who have been brought to America are daily becoming, under all the disadvantages of servitude, more ingenious and susceptible of instruction."

In theory, at any rate, Jefferson's conception of universal equality did not, and logically could not, exclude

* See S. K. Padover, "Benjamin Banneker: Unschooled Wizard," in *The New Republic,* February 2, 1948.

nonwhites. He may have had lingering doubts about the mental endowment and state of moral development of Negroes—and to the end of his life he doubted his own doubts—but this was no reason for denying them their rights, to which, as human beings, they were entitled at birth. The notion of natural rights was not built on ability, whether high or low. Talent, of whatever degree, was no measure of rights. If it were, there could be no popular or republican government, because only geniuses would then be entitled to rule. As Jefferson put it: "Because Sir Isaac Newton was superior to others in understanding, he was not therefore lord of the person or property of others." (*See Reading No. 50.*) About half a century later (*ca.* 1854), Abraham Lincoln used a similar argument in his devastating analysis of the illogic of slavery.*

The Agonizing Problem of Slavery. The whole question was, of course, complicated by the institution of slavery. For Jefferson, slavery was, as he put it, "a subject of early and tender consideration," which continued to trouble him all his life. As a freshman member of the House of Burgesses, to which he was elected at the age of 26, he had seconded a motion by Colonel Theodorick Bland, an able and experienced legislator, for the improvement of the lot of slaves. Although the motion was moderate, young Jefferson was dismayed by the fury which it aroused among his fellow legislators. In his old age he still recalled with a touch of bitterness how the gentlemanly Colonel Bland was denounced as "enemy of his country" and treated with the "grossest indecorum." But this did not affect Jefferson's basic antipathy to slavery.

In his second and third drafts of the Virginia Constitution (1776), Jefferson included the phrase: "No person

---

* Lincoln wrote: "If A can prove . . . that he may, of right, enslave B—why may not B snatch the same argument, and prove equally that he may enslave A? . . . You do not mean *color* exactly? You mean the whites are *intellectually* the superiors of the blacks, and do therefore have the right to enslave them? Take care. . . . By this rule, you are to be the slave to the first man you meet with an intellect superior to your own."

hereafter coming into this country shall be held . . . in slavery under any pretext whatever." In his *Notes on Virginia,* especially Query XIV, he excoriated slavery with matchless eloquence as a psychological taint and as a moral offense against God and man: "I tremble for my country when I reflect that God is just; that his justice cannot sleep forever." His draft for the *Government of the Western Territory* contained the all-important provision for the abolition of slavery and involuntary servitude in what were to become the states of the Middle West after the year 1800. (*See Reading No. 6.*)

Of the many plans suggested for the solution of slavery, Jefferson favored the one that combined emancipation and colonization. This provided for a training of young Negroes, girls up to the age of 18 and boys up to 21, in agriculture and other skills, at public expense, to be followed by their settlement at some proper place, presumably in Africa. The colonists were to be supplied with household goods, tools, seeds, and animals, and to be declared "a free and independent people" under American protection until they had acquired sufficient strength to be on their own. At the same time an equal number of white immigrants were to be encouraged to come to America as replacement for the Negroes.

To the question as to why the blacks should not be incorporated into the state, instead of going to all the trouble and expense of shipping one group out and bringing another one in, Jefferson replied that it was in practice impossible to do anything else. As things stood, feelings ran too high on the subject to permit any harmonious adjustment between blacks and whites on a level of equality. There was too much bias on the one side, and too much resentment on the other. "Deep-rooted prejudices entertained by the whites," Jefferson pointed out; "ten thousand recollections, by the blacks, of the injuries they have sustained," all this could only lead to further provocations, divisions, and convulsions that might end in the extermination of the one or the other race. (*See Reading No. 50.*)

Had Jefferson continued to be in the service of his native state, where slavery was an important institution, the search for a practical solution of the problem, he said would never have been out of sight for him. But more distant duties called. From the days of the American Revolution until 1809, he was occupied with other services and was, in fact, away from home much of the time. He did not finally return to Virginia until he was 66 years old, and by that time he did not feel that at his age—with his fortunes depleted and his estate encumbered by debt—he could undertake an antislavery movement. He kept hoping that the younger generation would do something about the "peculiar institution," but found to his dismay that little was being done. Southerners, in particular, seemed to be indifferent to the problem which to the aging Jefferson continued to be as alarming as a "fire-bell in the night."

The founding of Liberia, in Africa, by the American Colonization Society in 1822, more or less along Jefferson's own ideas, came too late to bring him much comfort. The enterprise was not, at any rate, a success in Africa, and in the United States the Negroes did not seem to be interested in it. And so Jefferson's last years continued to be perturbed by slavery. Personally, he had always been a kind and considerate master. He trained his slaves in various crafts and skills* and treated them "as well as white servants." (*See Reading No. 51.*) In his testament he provided for the emancipation of his personal slaves, but this did not affect the institution of slavery which filled him with forebodings. If the Southerners did not solve it, he said, they would be "the murderers of our own children." The year 1861 was to show that his fears were prophetic.

Attitude Towards Indians. In regard to the other minority group in the United States, the Indians, Jefferson's opinion differed from that which he held about Negroes. The social and economic positions of Indians and Negroes also differed, if for no other reason than that the former were free to roam in their wildernesses, gun, bow and arrow, or tomahawk in hand. The Negroes were enchained by slavery and forbidden to possess arms.

* For a slave's-eye view of Jefferson, see *Memoirs of a Monticello Slave, As Dictated to Charles Campbell in the 1840's, by Isaac, One of Thomas Jefferson's Slaves,* ed. by R. W. Logan (Charlottesville, Va., 1951).

All this may have affected Jefferson's conclusions about their respective characters. At any rate, he had no doubts about the Indians' intellectual or moral qualities. He admired them for their courage, their firmness of character, and their imagination. Their eloquence, he thought, was of the highest order and so was their mental endowment, at least potentially. Jefferson believed that Indians easily compared with Europeans at the same stage of historic development. "I am safe in affirming," he told a French friend, "that the proofs of genius given by the Indians of North America place them on a level with whites in the same uncultivated state."

The trouble with the Indians, Jefferson felt, was not intellectual or racial inferiority, but their mode of life. Their nomadic existence perpetuated their poverty, insecurity, and backwardness. Their hunting economy simply could not provide them with enough food and other necessities to enable them to make good progress in the arts of civilization. What was equally bad, was that their reliance upon the chase involved them in constant wars over possession of land, Indians bloodily defending their wild tracts as desperately needed animal preserves, and whites lusting after these tracts for farming.

Jefferson sympathized both with the plight of the Indians and the land hunger of the whites. He shared the latters' conviction that agriculture, and not hunting, was the true basis of progress and civilization. He, therefore, saw no solution but for the Indians to settle down and become like other Americans. In his many addresses to the chiefs of the Indian nations,* Jefferson, as President, urged upon them the wisdom and necessity of giving up their nomadism and taking up the peaceful pursuits of agriculture and animal husbandry. In time, he believed, this would lead the Indians to merge with the rest of the population. As he wrote in a letter of instructions to

* For a full collection of Jefferson's addresses to the Indian chiefs (the Wabash, Illinois, Miamis, Potawatomies, Delawares, Shawnees, Choctaws, Osages, Foxes, Sacs, Chickasaws, Creeks, Missouris, Sioux, Cherokees, Ricaras, Mandams, Kitchaos, Wyandottes, Senecas, Mohecans, etc.), see S. K. Padover, ed., *The Complete Jefferson* (1943), Ch. XII.

Colonel Benjamin Hawkins, the Federal Indian agent, the ultimate hope of stability and happiness for the Indians was to let their settlements "blend together" with those of the whites, "to intermix, and become one people." (*See Reading No. 52.*)

No Race Prejudice. In the light of later developments, it is possible to say that Jefferson underestimated the potentials of Negroes as he may have overestimated those of Indians. But this was not a matter of race prejudice or favoritism but, rather, one of insufficient information, which was, moreover, deflected by a special angle of observation. His doubts about Negroes were hazarded as guesses, hedged by contradicting qualifications, and never stated as firm, scientifically supported beliefs. Neither in his actions nor in his writings is there evidence to show that Jefferson meant to exclude men of color—any color or race—from his theory of universal equality. Nor is there any reason to doubt the sincerity of his lifelong belief in human brotherhood, as expressed in a statement he uttered at the age of 76: "I am ready to say to every human being 'thou art my brother' and to offer him the hand of concord and amity."

— 7 —

RELIGION AND
CHURCH-STATE SEPARATION

The Statute of Virginia for Religious Freedom, the second of the three acts of his life for which Jefferson wished to be remembered by posterity, marked a milestone in human liberty. As a philosophical libertarian, he was acutely aware that freedom of conscience was at the root of all other liberties. Once established, it freed the human mind from the shackles of fixed dogmas and hypnotizing rituals, and opened up the mind to the serene world of reason and rational happiness. For Jefferson, the battle for religious liberty was, therefore, of paramount importance.

The Virginia bill for religious freedom was passed by the Assembly in 1786, after a ten-year struggle, which Jefferson described as the "severest contest in which I have ever been engaged." It was more than a local Jeffersonian victory over an official religion supported by public taxation, as was the case with the Anglican Church in Virginia. The permanent separation of religion from government in what was then America's biggest and perhaps most influential state, combined with the eloquence of Jefferson's phrasing of the bill (*see Reading No. 5*), made its consequences reach beyond the confines of Virginia.

Refusal to Engage in Religious Debates. Jefferson's historic struggle for religious liberty in his native state, as well as his lifelong championship of separation of Church from State, were to earn him, among the conservative opponents of his politics, the reputation of being an "atheist" and an enemy of religion in general and Christianity in particular. The persistent accusation of

64

infidelism, which he took with philosophic equanimity, was undeserved. He had made it an unalterable policy never to indulge in public squabbles, especially in matters as prone to emotionalism as is religion, and hence rarely took the trouble to refute the charges of atheism and un-Christianity. A supremely rational man, he knew that religious faith was deeply embedded in human feeling and not easily dented by reason. It was also a matter of sacred privacy. In any case, he was sure that his clerical enemies, whom he characterized as *genus irritabilis vatum*, were irreconcilable. He felt, therefore, that his time could be more usefully employed in matters other than what he considered to be arid controversy.

Jefferson's Personal Faith. A proper understanding of Jefferson, however, requires an analysis of his true religious position, particularly since he himself considered the subject of first importance both spiritually and politically. His attitude towards religion is perhaps best viewed from three angles. One was his personal faith, or credo. The other was his critical opinion of organized religion, particularly the historic record of Christianity. The third was his public policy, which involved the unalterable maintenance of a "wall of separation" between Church and State. Each of these facets illuminates the others and meshes with them.

In his personal faith, Jefferson, together with such contemporaries as Ethan Allen and Benjamin Franklin, was a Deist, a believer in what the influential Lord Shaftesbury (1671-1713) called "natural religion." This was based on the scientific belief that there was vast order in the Universe, which could be comprehended by intelligence. In his ultimate faith, therefore, Jefferson was a rationalist. He believed in God, but it was not the Deity of the traditional Christians or Jews but, rather, a universal Being who created the laws and "machinery" of nature. On occasion, Jefferson used the word "God," but his basic idea was more truly expressed in the vocable "Creator." Sometimes it was the "benevolent Creator," or a similar equivalent.

An ardent believer in science (a term which also included what is today known as scholarship) and in the power of human reason to unlock the mysteries of the universe, as well as cure the maladies of mankind, Jefferson was convinced that in nature there was a logic based on immutable universal laws. Reason had to assume that this logical universe ("laws of nature") was the creation of a Supreme Architect, whom many called Deity. Despite the voluminous writings and dogmatic assertions of theologians, the rationalist in Jefferson could not accept the creedal claims that the ways and intentions of the Supreme Architect, or Creator, were clearly, fixedly, and unequivocally known to man. To Jefferson, His ways were endlessly mysterious, and as a scientific mind he modestly preferred to suspend judgment until verification was possible. For this reason he eschewed metaphysical questions. To a clergyman who asked his opinion about the other-world of spirits, Jefferson replied with gentle irony that he chose to repose his head on "that pillow of ignorance" which a "benevolent Creator" had made so soft for us, because He knew that we should be forced to use it often.

Jefferson was brought up in the Church of England, to which his parents belonged, and from childhood on he was familiar with its liturgy, hymns, psalms and, of course, the magnificent King James' Version of the Bible. But as an adult he was not an active church member, saying that the clergyman knew no more the way to heaven than did the layman. Clerical vestment, he felt, was no guarantee of knowledge or wisdom. Truth could be found outside ecclesiastical organizations or elaborate theologies, for which in any case he had scant sympathy. Jefferson's faith was altogether a personal one, and he seemed to have no need for a church to buttress it. It was one of his unshakable principles that religious belief was an absolutely private affair, not to be violated by government or pried into by neighbors. Religion, he said again and again, was entirely a matter between "every man and his Maker," in which nobody—neither public nor private groups—had any right whatsoever to "intermeddle."

Jefferson's private faith was that of a rationalist and moralist. He believed in reason and in goodness. He rejected the convoluted theological underpinnings of historical Christianity as contrary to rationality and hostile to morality, as well as to freedom. "In every country and in every age," he wrote, "the priest has been hostile to liberty." Jefferson did not consider it paradoxical to accept the founder of Christianity but not the elaborate ecclesiastical institutions that, for some 1,700 years, had proliferated around and in the name of Jesus.

Admiration for Jesus. Jefferson regarded Jesus as a great, perhaps the greatest, moral teacher, a human reformer who had attempted to restore the Jewish religion to the principles of "pure deism" and to more just notions of the attributes of God. But he felt that the purity of the Nazarene's ideas had been perverted by the priests and the theologians. As he told his friend Benjamin Rush (April 21, 1803), "to the corruptions of Christianity I am indeed opposed; but not to the genuine precepts of Jesus himself." In the sense that he sincerely followed the commanding moral doctrines of Jesus, Jefferson called himself a "real Christian."

To Jefferson it was clear, as he stated in his *Syllabus of the Doctrines of Jesus* (1803) and other writings, that Jesus' "excellence" lay in his towering humanness, rather than in a divineness which "he never claimed." Jefferson was not with Jesus in all his doctrines. He differed in some things, as he confided to his friend and one-time secretary William Short: "I am a materialist; he takes the side of spiritualism; he preaches the efficacy of repentance towards forgiveness of sin; I require a counterpoise of good works to redeem it." But altogether, he felt, the purity, the morality, and the eloquence of Jesus were unmatched.

In his retirement, Jefferson cut out the moral precepts as reported in the Gospel and rearranged them, in four parallel columns (Greek, Latin, French, English), so as to make a coherent whole. These "fragments," constituting a supreme code of morals, were published, almost a century later, under the title of *The Life and Morals of Jesus of Nazareth* (1904). Commonly known as *The Jefferson Bible*, it has been republished in later editions.*

* For a recent edition, containing photostated pages of Jefferson's original four-column arrangement, see O. I. A. Roche, ed., *The Jefferson Bible, with the Annotated Commentaries on Religion of Thomas Jefferson* (1964).

Admiration for Other Spiritual Leaders. Next to Jesus, Jefferson cherished other noble leaders of the human spirit and the free mind, particularly the great moralists. Among those he most admired were Socrates (but not Plato, for whose "foggy mysticisms" he had a strong antipathy), Seneca, Epicurus, and Epictetus, to whom he referred as "our master." (*See Reading No. 53.*) There are no references to Buddha or Confucius in Jefferson's moral cosmos, but only because his education, like that of his American and European contemporaries, was almost entirely Occidental. In Jefferson's time, the Orient and its philosophy were still largely unexplored territory.

His Universal Tolerance. Jefferson's personal religion, rooted in what he called rational moral philosophy, contained no room for intolerance. His faith was undogmatic and uncompulsive, having no emotional need either to convert or to persecute. Always insisting that religion was "a concern purely between our God and our consciences," Jefferson held that the souls of others should be respected and not obtruded. For himself, he informed Mrs. Samuel Harrison Smith, whose husband was the editor of the pro-Jeffersonian *National Intelligencer,* he never told anybody his own religion nor scrutinized that of another: "I never attempted to make a convert, nor wish to change another's creed." He added that he judged men's religion by the lives they led, and not by their doctrines.

In all matters of the human spirit, Jefferson was openminded and relaxed. This was not "tolerance" in the crude sense of the term. It was, rather, a deep respect for the human individual and his dignity. So far as he was concerned, anyone and everyone was free—and, indeed, had a natural right—to believe or disbelieve whatever he wished, so long as he did not thereby inflict harm on others. As he put it with rare bluntness in the *Notes on Virginia:* "*It does me no injury for my neighbor to say there are twenty gods, or no God. It neither picks my pocket nor breaks my leg.*" (*See Reading No. 54B.*)

No Church Affiliation. Jefferson's faith, with its underlying secular morality and belief in a Creator, has made Unitarians, with a certain measure of justification, claim him as one of them. He was, in fact, a friend and admirer of Dr. Joseph Priestley, the scientist who founded Unitarianism. Jefferson wrote in his old age that he hoped that there was not a young man now living in the United States who would not die a Unitarian. But Jefferson did not affiliate with that or any other religious institution. In this matter too, he was, like the later Ralph Waldo Emerson, a complete individualist. "If I could not go to heaven but with a party," Jefferson said, "I would not go there at all." One of his favorite stories was that of the eloquent Quaker preacher who shocked his audience by exclaiming that there was not a Quaker, Presbyterian, Methodist, or Baptist in heaven—and then quickly reassured his hearers by adding that in heaven God knew no distinctions, but considered all good men as His children and as brothers of the same human family.

Reason Behind Church-State Separation. Jefferson's criticism of institutionalized religion as tied to government—not of religion itself—was political and moral, rather than theological. He did, in fact, eschew doctrinal disputes. His argument against any church-government alliance was twofold: It was a violation of natural rights, and it was inimical to freedom.

Under the theory of natural rights, government had no authority in the field of faith. Men, Jefferson wrote, had never submitted the rights of conscience to their rulers and could, indeed, never do so, because "we are answerable for them to our God" only. The legitimate powers of government extend solely to acts injurious to others, but not to the area of belief. (*See Reading No. 54B.*) When government moves into the realm of conscience, it violates men's fundamental rights and, in the process, destroys freedom.

History, particularly that of Christendom, was replete with examples illustrating the evil effects of governmental coercion in matters of religion. In this regard, Jefferson saw no distinction between the intolerances of the various Western faiths. Despite his own Protestant origins, he disliked John Calvin ("he was an atheist . . . , his religion was daemonism") as strongly as he did any Roman Catholic Inquisitor. In principle, he could see little difference between the burning of Michael Servetus or

Salem witches by Protestants and the *autos-da-fé* of the Spanish Inquisitors. They were all detestable, and he considered them deadly enemies of mankind.

Christendom's Historic Intolerance. In the *Notes on Virginia,* where he discussed extensively his ideas of religious freedom and toleration, Jefferson asked the rhetorical question: "Why have Christians been distinguished above all people who have ever lived for persecutions?" It was not Christianity itself, for as a religion it preached brotherly love rather than hate. His answer was that the reason for Christendom's unremitting intolerance and continuous persecutions—the Albigensian Crusades, the Holy Inquisitions, the Lutheran extirpation of peasants, the unending pogroms on Jews, the burning of "heretics"—was the alliance between Church and State. The unholy union began with the edict of Emperor Theodosius I in A.D. 380 (decreeing that the opponents of the Church "be branded with the ignominious name of heretics" and then be handed over to the "chastisement" and "punishment" of the secular authority) and continued, in virtually all European communities, into Jefferson's day. He called it a "loathsome" combination.

To Jefferson, as also to men like James Madison and other founders of the American Constitution, it was axiomatic that any union of ecclesiastical authority with political power—anywhere—always spelled tyranny. Wherever Church and State combined, the two (known in medieval terminology as the "two swords," one being the secular power and the other the "sacred authority" of the priests) cooperated to maintain a universal spirit of oppression. As Jefferson put it, cleric and despot nourished each other's privileged position, the one fettering the mind and the other enslaving the body. Through terror and torture, they battened upon the people, and neither freedom nor happiness had a chance so long as the two were in union.

Christendom's historic policy of coercion in the field of religion and its systematic extirpation and persecution of creedal opponents, Jefferson felt, was as futile as it was cruel. It simply did not achieve its objectives—uniformity and obedience—which Jefferson regarded as both undesirable and impossible. "Millions of innocent men, women and children, since the introduction of Christianity," he wrote, "have been burnt, tortured, fined, imprisoned, yet we have not advanced one inch towards uniformity." (*See Reading No. 54.*) In the long run, he felt, no amount of tyrannical effort can make humanity fit into the bed of Procrustes.

Church-State Separation Essential to Freedom and Happiness. For freedom and happiness, Jefferson was convinced, a severance between Church and State was an absolute necessity. It was essential both for religion and for politics. For in any close union between ecclesiastical and governmental establishments, each corrupted the other. Jefferson believed that the very essence of religion was degraded when the secular power was used to impose faith or spiritual ideas on persons who, deep in their hearts, did not believe in them. Coercion for the sake of trying to achieve uniformity was bad for religion and worse for society. It made people either hypocrites or fools, Jefferson said. "Nothing but free discussion," he wrote, could preserve the purity of religion and the dignity of man. Genuine religion could be maintained only through the free volition of the individual, giving no ruler or organized body the right to "intermeddle" in the sacred privacy of personal belief. Furthermore, the human mind, in all secular activities, notably scientific inquiries and political pursuits, could be kept both free and creative only if the combined coercions of ecclesiastical and governmental organizations were permanently eliminated.

His Policy of Absolute Church-State Separation. Freedom on all levels, therefore, made it imperative to divorce religion from politics. Each, religious institutions and political power, was to be set absolutely free from the other, for the benefit both of man's individual spirit and society's common health. Through a binding constitutional and legal separation of Church and State, the tragedies, sufferings, and degradations of European Christendom would be avoided in America, and man's spirit would be once and for all liberated for the pursuit of freedom and happiness.

Such was the thinking behind Jefferson's *Statute for*

Religious Freedom, as well as the rationale underlying the Bill of Rights of the Federal Constitution, especially the First Amendment, drafted by his devoted friend James Madison.

In his public policy, Jefferson was unbending in maintaining what he called the "wall of separation" between Church and State. He hailed the freedom that resulted from it in his First and Second Inaugural Addresses and in other utterances. To him, the principle of separation was absolute, allowing for no compromises. He was sharply critical of those who mixed politics with religion or who preached partisanship from the pulpit.

As President, he refused to issue proclamations that had any connection with church matters. When the Reverend Samuel Miller asked him to recommend a day of fasting and prayer, Jefferson replied sternly: "I consider the government of the United States as interdicted by the Constitution from intermeddling with religious institutions, their doctrines, disciplines, or exercises." (*See Reading No. 55.*) When he founded the University of Virginia, he deliberately made no provision for a professorship of divinity, but suggested that religious instruction be given nearby—"but always understanding that these schools shall be independent of the University."

The Jeffersonian ideal of Church-State separation, with its resultant religious freedom, has been the cornerstone of American democracy. He himself called it the "most inestimable of our blessings," and in retrospect he was right. Thanks to the separation, Americans have enjoyed religious liberty to an unprecedented degree. They have also escaped the systematic violence resulting from religious coercion. The United States has, in fact, been singularly free from the horrors of persecution and oppression that had disfigured the moral face of European countries for a thousand years and more.

Jefferson's "wall of separation" has been breached in spots. The general structure, however, still stands. In recent years, it has been given new support, in virtually Jeffersonian language, by the United States Supreme Court. (See especially *Abington School District v. Schempp; Murray v. Curlett:* June 17, 1963.) So long as

e wall stands, freedom, as Jefferson conceived it, remains
fe. But a Jeffersonian alertness to attempted breaches—
exemplified by Justice Hugo Black, to whom the Bill of
ights is an "absolute"*—is imperative for the citizenry
large.

"It is my belief that there *are* 'absolutes' in our Bill of
Rights, and that they were put there on purpose by men
who knew what words meant, and meant their prohibi-
tions to be 'absolutes.' . . . Today most Americans seem
to have forgotten the ancient evils which forced their
ancestors to flee to this new country and to form a government stripped of old powers used to oppress them. But
the Americans who supported the Revolution and the
adoption of our Constitution knew firsthand the dangers
of tyrannical government. They were familiar with the
long existing practice of English persecutions of people
wholly because of their religious or political beliefs. . . .
The First Amendment is truly the heart of the Bill of
Rights." Justice Hugo Black, "The Bill of Rights and
the Federal Government," in E. Cahn, ed., *The Great
Rights* (1963), pp. 45-63.

— 8 —

EDUCATION AND HAPPINESS

The Importance of Education to Freedom. In the Spring of 1825, when the University of Virginia opened, Jefferson felt that he had culminated his career by the creation of a center where liberty and learning would be preserved as a "holy charge." He was quietly elated. He wrote to his friend, Judge Augustus B. Woodward, the planner of the University of Michigan (which he called "Catholepistemiad of Michigania"), that he was closing the last scenes of his life by fashioning an institution that would have a permanent influence on the virtue, freedom, and happiness of "those who are to come after us."

For Jefferson, education for the people had been a lifelong preoccupation. It was a golden thread that ran through his whole political and social thought. For he was convinced that without a reasonably educated people there could be no liberty. Ignorance and freedom were natural enemies. You could, he held, have one or the other, but never both at the same time. "If a nation," he wrote, "expects to be ignorant and free, in a state of civilization, it expects what never was and never will be." This was a point he made repeatedly over the years. So far as he was concerned, the cost of education, especially public schools for the common people, did not matter. It was beyond price.

All over the world, aristocrats and monarchs had always had a monopoly on education for themselves. They did not have to provide it for others, because only they, the elite, had the power to rule and to make decisions. The people in general were deliberately kept in ignorance, Jefferson believed, so as to be more easily dominated by their rulers.

74

A republic, however, had different requirements. It was not centered around a ruling class, but was rooted in the people—the "ultimate guardians of their own liberty." But illiterates could not be expected to know how to govern. To rule, even indirectly, meant to make choices, and to make choices required knowledge which, at least in a state of civilization, could be acquired primarily through schools that were open and available to everybody. Jefferson thus considered education the only "sure foundation" for the maintenance of a republic and the preservation of freedom. (*See Reading No. 56.*) He saw, in fact, no alternative. In his First Inaugural Address, he called education one of the "essential principles of our government."

The Bill for the . . . Diffusion of Knowledge. Jefferson began to make educational plans when he was still a young legislator. In his capacity as Revisor (together with the distinguished jurists, George Wythe and Edmund Pendleton) of Virginia's legal code, he had drafted three bills in the field of education which were pioneer steps in the promotion of his ideal of a commonwealth of freedom. Of the three,* "A Bill for the More General Diffusion of Knowledge" (No. 79), which he completed sometime in December 1778, was of special significance. It was a blueprint for a public school system in Virginia that was to serve, with modifications, as a model and example for the rest of the country.

Jefferson's Bill for the "Diffusion of Knowledge" provided for a division of every county into five- or six-square-mile districts, called "hundreds," in each of which there was to be built a free three-year school for teaching all children reading, writing, and arithmetic. Every year, after a diligent and impartial examination, the boy of "best genius" was to be selected for further education in Greek, Latin, geography, and higher arithmetic, without cost to his parents. There were to be 20 such boys chosen

* The other two were: "A Bill for Amending the Constitution of the College of William and Mary" (No. 80), and "A Bill for Establishing a Public Library" (No. 81). For the whole collection of Bills, a total of 126, see J. P. Boyd, ed., *The Papers of Thomas Jefferson,* II (1950), pp. 305-664.

annually. After six years, the superior half of this group
—those of the "best learning and most hopeful genius
and disposition"—were to be selected and sent to William
and Mary College. There, at liberty to study "such
sciences as they shall choose," they were to be "educated,
boarded, and clothed" for three years, at public expense.

The Uses of History. Jefferson's educational plan
was designed to achieve four major objectives. First, it
was to make all people literate—at least in the traditional
three R's—and thereby make it possible for them to rule
themselves intelligently. For this purpose, he proposed
that the first stages of education emphasize mainly historical readings. He accepted the famous dictum of
Dionysius of Halicarnassus (*ca*. 20 B.C.), repeated by
(and often given sole credit to) Lord Bolingbroke in
the eighteenth century, that "History is philosophy teaching by examples." In Jefferson's rephrasing, history was a
subject which, "by apprising the people of the past, en-
ables them to judge the future." It was a reservoir of
indispensable political lessons. A proper knowledge of
history," Jefferson believed, would furnish a self-governing people with the necessary yardsticks for judging what
was right and for defeating what was wicked in their
polity. (*See Reading No. 57.*)

Scientific Training. Secondly, the Bill for the "Diffusion of Knowledge" would assure training at higher
levels, both for the sake of science itself and for leadership in general. Jefferson considered the promotion of
science (and scholarship) as the noblest of human en-
deavors. He thought it inconceivable, for example, that
a genius like Sir Isaac Newton should ever have been
wasted on political, or any other nonscientific, occupa-
tions. A scientist of such calibre was nature's most precious gift to man. So was talent in general. Jefferson
believed that talent, which could be found scattered
among all classes of the population, was nature's chief
instrument for the progress and amelioration of the human condition. It was, therefore, the duty and the interest
of society to encourage and develop talent to every possible extent.

The selection and training of gifted young men, at
public expense, would furnish invaluable leadership for

the "instruction, the trusts, and government of society."
(*See Reading No. 47.*) They would constitute a desirable
"natural aristocracy," based on tested ability, rather than,
as in Europe, social status or money. In other countries,
Jefferson pointed out, the "mass of talents" lay "buried
in poverty," and thus lost to the people for lack of educational opportunities. In America, public-supported education would bring forth and nourish the gifted for the
benefit of all.

Training in Virtue: To Avoid Corruption. The third
reason for Jefferson's championship of public education,
closely connected with the first, was the need for the inculcation and maintenance of "virtue" among the people.
He assumed the correctness of Montesquieu's observation that the essential principle of a republic was "virtue."
To Jefferson, the term was practically interchangeable
with morality. He used the word in the context of hon-
esty, simplicity, kindliness, and benevolence. "The essence
of virtue," he remarked in a letter to John Adams, "is in
doing good to others."

A republic needed virtue in its citizens, because without it there could be no enduring self-government, since
the latter was based on mutual confidence and respect for
others. It meant, among other things, simple human trust
in the majority—that it would not abuse the minority,
which was often helpless. A degraded people—one without virtue, that is, without kindliness and consideration
for others—obviously could not govern, itself or others,
except through violence and brutality.

Jefferson, despite his over-all optimism regarding man's
nature, nevertheless had a lurking fear of the possibility
of corruption in the human species. Men, he knew, were
not angels. History was full of examples of how people
could be debased and put to vicious use by corrupt leaders. "In every government on earth," he pointed out in
the *Notes on Virginia,* "there is some trace of human
weakness, some germ of corruption and degeneracy,"
which cunning will discover and wickedness open for
exploitation.

To guard against such a potential "gangrene" in the
body politic, it was necessary to instill virtuous ideas in
the minds of the citizens. This could be done by example

and by precept. But the steadiest and most reliable instruments for the inculcation of virtue were schools and books. For this reason, Jefferson recommended any good reading, including fiction, provided that the novels portrayed decent characters and presented salutary examples. "Everything," he said, "is useful which contributes to fix us in the principles and practices of virtue."

Education to Achieve Happiness. The fourth and possibly most important reason for Jefferson's espousal of the "diffusion of knowledge among the people" was his conviction that it was an indispensable vehicle for the achievement of happiness. He viewed happiness, not in the modern sense of "fun" or "good time," but as personal fulfillment expressing itself in an atmosphere of political freedom. Happiness was an inner state that derived from good conscience and satisfying occupation and did not depend upon status or affluence.

For Jefferson it was unthinkable that ignorant people could be happy, any more than they could be free. Contrary to the proverb, ignorance was the reverse of bliss. The uneducated could not attain happiness because they remained in a state of brutishness, their minds filled with frightening superstitions, instead of liberating truth. Hence they were always easily exploited and dominated, and thus unable to achieve the serenity and self-fulfillment that constituted happiness, without which, Jefferson believed, life was not worth living. The fetters could be broken only by knowledge that comes through education. If you enlighten the people, Jefferson told Dupont de Nemours, you will find that their oppressions of body and mind "will vanish like evil spirits at the dawn of day."

Jefferson may have been too optimistic about the wonderful consequences that he expected to flow from the "blessings of instruction." But it was his abiding faith that widespread education, together with freedom, would advance the "happiness of the human race." (*See Reading No. 58.*) And in his philosophy, that was the sole object of all legitimate government. Could there be a nobler ideal?

— Reading No. 1 —

JEFFERSON'S EDUCATION AT WILLIAM AND MARY*

There are scattered autobiographic recollections in Jefferson's letters and in the "loose scraps" of political notes known as The Anas *(1791-1806), but the most consistent account of himself is the relatively brief* Autobiography, *which he began—"for the information of my family"— at the age of 77. The* Autobiography *does not cover his whole life. It begins with the origins of his father's family (Wales) and ends early in 1790, when he arrived in New York City to serve as George Washington's Secretary of State.*

On the death of my father I went to the Rev'd [*James*] Maury, a correct classical scholar, with whom I continued two years, and then went to William and Mary College, to wit in the spring of 1760, where I continued two years. It was my great good fortune, and what probably fixed the destinies of my life, that Dr. William Small of Scotland was then professor of mathematics, a man profound in most of the useful branches of science, with a happy talent of communication, correct and gentlemanly manners, & an enlarged & liberal mind. He, most happily for me, became soon attached to me & made me his daily companion when not engaged in the school; and from his conversation I got my first views of the expansion of science & of the system of things in which we are placed. . . . He was the first who ever gave in that college regu-

* *Autobiography* (1821). Published in P. L. Ford, ed., *The Writings of Thomas Jefferson,* I (1892), pp. 3-4.

lar lectures in Ethics, Rhetoric & Belles Lettres. He returned to Europe in 1762, having previously filled up the measure of his goodness to me, by procuring for me, from his most intimate friend G. Wythe, a reception as a student of law, under his direction, and introduced me to the acquaintance and familiar table of Governor [*Francis*] Fauquier, the ablest man who had ever filled that office. With him, and at his table, Dr. Small & Mr. Wythe, his *amici omnium horarum,* & myself, formed a *partie quarrée,* & to the habitual conversations on these occasions I owed much instruction. Mr. Wythe continued to be my faithful and beloved Mentor in youth, and my most affectionate friend through life. In 1767, he led me into the practice of the law at the bar of the General Court.

— Reading No. 2 —

THE ORIGINAL RIGHTS
OF AMERICANS*

In his Autobiography, *Jefferson writes that, after the Governor of Virginia had dissolved the House of Burgesses (May 20, 1774), he prepared notes to serve as instructions for the newly elected Convention. "They printed the paper . . . and gave it the title of* A Summary View. . . . *In this form it got to London, where the opposition took it up, shaped it to opposition views, and, in that form, it ran rapidly through several editions." The pamphlet made Jefferson's reputation.*

↑   ↑   ↑

Resolved that . . . an humble and dutiful address be presented to His Majesty, begging leave to lay before him . . . the united complaints of His Majesty's subjects in America; complaints which are excited by many unwarrantable incroachments and usurpations . . . by the legislature of one part of the empire, upon those rights which God and the laws have given equally and independently to all. . . .

To remind him that our ancestors, before their emigration to America, were the free inhabitants of the British dominions in Europe, and possessed a right, which nature has given to all men, of departing from the country in

* A Summary View of the Rights of British America, August, 1774. Published in P. L. Ford, ed., The Writings of Thomas Jefferson, I (1892), pp. 421-447; also in J. P. Boyd, ed., The Papers of Thomas Jefferson, I (1950), pp. 121-135; S. K. Padover, ed., The Complete Jefferson (1943), pp. 6-19.

which chance, not choice has placed them, of going in quest of new habitations, and of there establishing new societies, under such laws and regulations as to them shall seem most likely to promote public happiness. . . .

Open your breast, Sire, to liberal and expanded thought. Let not the name of George the Third be a blot in the page of history. . . . Deal out to all equal and impartial right. Let no act be passed by any one legislature which may infringe on the rights and liberties of another. . . . This, Sire, is the advice of your great American council. . . . The God who gave us life, gave us liberty at the same time; the hand of force may destroy, but cannot disjoin them.

— Reading No. 3 —

BACKGROUND OF THE DECLARATION OF INDEPENDENCE

After the Continental Congress adopted Richard Henry Lee's famous motion, made on June 7, 1776, that "these United Colonies are & of right ought to be free & independent States," Jefferson was appointed to the committee to draft a statement on independence. The other members of the committee—John Adams, Benjamin Franklin, Robert R. Livingston, and Roger Sherman—were older and more famous, but the 33-year-old Jefferson was chosen draftsman because of his reputation as a fine writer. That reputation rested largely on his authorship of A Summary View of the Rights of British America. *(See Reading No. 2.) Jefferson worked on the draft of the Declaration of Independence between June 11 and June 28. By July 4 the Congress finally adopted it, with a few relatively minor changes. In these selections Jefferson explains some of the background and meaning of the Declaration.*

✓   ✓   ✓

A.*

The committee of five met; no such thing as a subcommittee was proposed, but they unanimously pressed on myself alone to undertake the draught. I consented; I drew it; but before I reported it to the committee, I

---

* Letter to James Madison, August 30, 1823. Published in P. L. Ford, ed., *The Writings of Thomas Jefferson,* X (1899), pp. 267-268.

communicated it *separately* to Dr. Franklin and Mr. Adams, requesting their corrections, because they were the two members whose judgments and amendments I wished most to have the benefit, before presenting it to the committee; and you have seen the original paper now in my hands, with the corrections of Dr. Franklin and Mr. Adams interlined in their own hand writings. Their alterations were two or three only, and merely verbal. I then wrote a fair copy, reported it to the committee, and from them, unaltered, to Congress. This personal communication and consultation with Mr. Adams, he has misremembered into the actings of a sub-committee. Pickering's observation. . . , 'that it contained no new ideas. . . ,' may all be true. Of that I am not to be the judge. Richard Henry Lee charged it as copied from Locke's Treatise on Government. . . . Whether I had gathered my ideas from reading or reflection I do not know. I know only that I turned to neither book nor pamphlet while writing it. I did not consider it as any part of my charge to invent new ideas altogether, and to offer no sentiment which had ever been expressed before.

B.*

With respect to our rights, and the acts of the British government contravening those rights, there was but one opinion on this side of the water. All American Whigs thought alike on these subjects. When forced, therefore, to resort to arms for redress, and appeal to the tribunal of the world was deemed proper for our justification. This was the object of the Declaration of Independence. Not to find out new principles, or new arguments, never before thought of, not merely to say things which had never been said before; but to place before mankind the common sense of the subject, in terms so plain and firm as to command their assent, and to justify ourselves in the independent stand we are compelled to take. Neither aiming at originality of principle or sentiment, nor yet copied from any particular and previous writing, it was intended to be an expression of the American mind, and

* Letter to Henry Lee, May 8, 1825. Published in P. L. Ford, ed., *The Writings of Thomas Jefferson*, X (1899), p. 343.

to give to that expression the proper tone and spirit called for by the occasion. All its authority rests then on the harmonizing sentiments of the day, whether expressed in conversation, in letters, printed essays, or in the elementary books of public right, as Aristotle, Cicero, Locke, Sidney, etc.

— Reading No. 4 —

A SELECTION FROM
THE DECLARATION
OF INDEPENDENCE*

When in the Course of human events, it becomes necessary for one people to dissolve the political bands which have connected them with another, and to assume among the powers of the earth, the separate and equal station to which the Laws of Nature and of Nature's God entitle them, a decent respect to the opinions of mankind requires that they should declare the causes which impel them to the separation. We hold these truths to be self-evident, that all men are created equal, that they are endowed by their Creator with certain unalienable Rights, that among these are Life, Liberty and the pursuit of Happiness. That to secure these rights, Governments are instituted among Men, deriving their just powers from the consent of the governed, That whenever any Form of Government becomes destructive of these ends, it is the Right of the People to alter or to abolish it, and to institute new Government, laying its foundation on such principles and organizing its powers in such form, as to them shall seem most likely to effect their Safety and Happiness. Prudence, indeed, will dictate that Governments long

* The Declaration of Independence is found not only in all the collected writings of Jefferson but in so many other publications and separate editions that it is unnecessary to cite a special reference. Those, however, who are interested in the evolution of the original text and the various drafts, should consult J. P. Boyd, ed., *The Papers of Thomas Jefferson*, I (1950), pp. 413-432.

established should not be changed for light and transient causes; and accordingly all experience hath shewn, that mankind are more disposed to suffer, while evils are sufferable, than to right themselves by abolishing the forms to which they are accustomed. But when a long train of abuses and usurpations, pursuing invariably the same Object evinces a design to reduce them under absolute Despotism, it is their right, it is their duty, to throw off such Government, and to provide new Guards for their future security. . . .

We, therefore, the Representatives of the United States of America, in General Congress, Assembled, appealing to the Supreme Judge of the world for the rectitude of our intentions, do, in the Name, and by Authority of the good People of these Colonies, solemnly publish and declare, That these United Colonies are, and of Right ought to be Free and Independent States; that they are absolved from all Allegiance to the British Crown, and that all political connection between them and the State of Great Britain, is and ought to be totally dissolved; and that as Free and Independent States, they have full Power to levy War, conclude Peace, contract Alliances, establish Commerce, and to do all other Acts and Things which Independent States may of right do. And for the support of this Declaration, with a firm reliance on the protection of divine Providence, we mutually pledge to each other our Lives, our Fortunes and our sacred Honor.

— Reading No. 5 —

A BILL FOR ESTABLISHING RELIGIOUS FREEDOM, 1779*[1]

SECTION I. Well aware that the opinions and belief of men depend on their own will, but follow involuntarily the evidence proposed to their minds; that Almighty God hath created the mind free, and manifested his supreme will that free it shall remain by making it altogether insusceptible of restraint; that all attempts to influence it by temporal punishments, or burthens, or by civil incapacitations, tend only to beget habits of hypocrisy and meanness, and are a departure from the plan of the holy author of our religion, who being lord both of body and mind, yet chose not to propagate it by coercions on either, as

* Published in P. L. Ford, ed., *The Writings of Thomas Jefferson*, II (1893), pp. 237-239; also in S. K. Padover, ed., *The Complete Jefferson* (1943). pp. 946-947.
[1] This constitutes Ch. LXXXII of the *Report of the Revisors*. The bill was introduced into the Virginia Assembly on June 13, 1779, and aroused so much opposition that its passage was delayed until 1786, when it was adopted with certain changes.

Jefferson considered this bill one of his major achievements; before he died, he asked that it be engraved on his tombstone that he was its author. Together with the Declaration of Independence, this bill does, indeed, rank as one of the great foundation stones of the American republic. It established religious freedom—the greatest of all freedoms—and toleration in Virginia, the most populous and influential American State, and served as a model for the rest of the country.

The bill was printed in Paris, in 1786, both in English and in French.

was in his Almighty power to do, but to exalt it by its
influence on reason alone; that the impious presumption
of legislature and ruler, civil as well as ecclesiastical, who,
being themselves but fallible and uninspired men, have
assumed dominion over the faith of others, setting up
their own opinions and modes of thinking as the only true
and infallible, and as such endeavoring to impose them on
others, hath established and maintained false religions
over the greatest part of the world and through all time:
That to compel a man to furnish contributions of money
for the propagation of opinions which he disbelieves and
abhors, is sinful and tyrannical; that even the forcing him
to support this or that teacher of his own religious persuasion, is depriving him of the comfortable liberty of
giving his contributions to the particular pastor whose
morals he would make his pattern, and whose powers he
feels most persuasive to righteousness; and is withdrawing
from the ministry those temporary rewards, which pro-
ceeding from an approbation of their personal conduct,
are an additional incitement to earnest and unremitting
labours for the instruction of mankind; that our civil
rights have no dependence on our religious opinions, any
more than our opinions in physics or geometry; and therefore the proscribing any citizen as unworthy the public
confidence by laying upon him an incapacity of being
called to offices of trust or emolument, unless he profess
or renounce this or that religious opinion, is depriving him
injudiciously of those privileges and advantages to which,
in common with his fellow-citizens, he has a natural right;
that it tends also to corrupt the principles of that very
religion it is meant to encourage, by bribing with a
monopoly of worldly honours and emoluments, those who
will externally profess and conform to it; that though
indeed these are criminals who do not withstand such
temptation, yet neither are those innocent who lay the
bait in their way; that the opinions of men are not the
object of civil government, nor under its jurisdiction; that
to suffer the civil magistrate to intrude his powers into
the field of opinion and to restrain the profession or
propagation of principles on supposition of their ill tendency is a dangerous fallacy, which at once destroys all
religious liberty, because he being of course judge of that

tendency will make his opinions the rule of judgment, and approve or condemn the sentiments of others only as they shall square with or suffer from his own; that it is time enough for the rightful purposes of civil government for its officers to interfere when principles break out into overt acts against peace and good order; and finally, that truth is great and will prevail if left to herself; that she is the proper and sufficient antagonist to error, and has nothing to fear from the conflict unless by human interposition disarmed of her natural weapons, free argument and debate; errors ceasing to be dangerous when it is permitted freely to contradict them.

SECTION II. We the General Assembly of Virginia do enact that no man shall be compelled to frequent or support any religious worship, place, or ministry whatsoever, nor shall be enforced, restrained, molested, or burthened in his body or goods, or shall otherwise suffer, on account of his religious opinions or belief; but that all men shall be free to profess, and by argument to maintain, their opinions in matters of religion, and that the same shall in no wise diminish, enlarge, or affect their civil capacities.

SECTION III. And though we well know that this Assembly, elected by the people for their ordinary purposes of legislation only, have no power to restrain the acts of succeeding Assemblies, constituted with powers equal to our own, and that therefore to declare this act to be irrevocable would be of no effect in law; yet we are free to declare, and do declare, that the rights hereby asserted are of the natural rights of mankind, and that if any act shall be hereafter passed to repeal the present or to narrow its operations, such act will be an infringement of natural right.

— Reading No. 6 —

REPORT ON GOVERNMENT FOR WESTERN TERRITORY*

As a member of the Congress of the Confederation, in 1783-1784, Jefferson drafted a plan for the government of the territory, both Northern and Southern, between the Ohio and Mississippi Rivers. One clause provided for the abolition of slavery after 1800, but it was defeated by a vote of 7 to 6. Had it passed, the Civil War might well have been avoided. After the defeat of the measure by a single vote, Jefferson exclaimed prophetically: "Thus we see the fate of millions unborn hanging on the tongue of one man, and Heaven was silent in that awful moment." Jefferson's basic ideas, however, including the abolition of slavery, were adopted in the 1787 Ordinance for the government of the Northwestern Territory.

✓ ✓ ✓

Resolved . . . that . . . temporary government shall only continue in force in any state until it shall have acquired 20,00 free inhabitants, when . . . they shall receive from [*Congress*] . . . authority . . . to establish a permanent Constitution & Government for themselves.

Provided that both the temporary & permanent Governments be established on these principles as their basis 1. That they shall forever remain a part of the United States of America. 2. That in their persons, property & territory, they shall be subject to the Government of the

* March 1, 1784. Text in P. L. Ford, ed., *The Writings of Thomas Jefferson,* III (1894), pp. 408-409; and in H. S. Randall, *The Life of Thomas Jefferson,* I (1857), pp. 397-398.

United States in Congress assembled and to the Articles of Confederation in all those cases in which the original States shall be so subject. 3. That they shall be subject to pay a part of the Federal debts contracted or to be contracted to be apportioned on them by Congress, according to the same common rule and measure by which apportionments thereof shall be made on the other States. 4. That their respective Governments shall be in republican forms, and shall admit no person to be a citizen, who holds any hereditary title. 5. That after the year 1800 of the Christian era, there shall be neither slavery nor involuntary servitude in any of the said states, otherwise than in punishment of crimes, whereof the party shall have been duly convicted to have been personally guilty.

— Reading No. 7 —

ADVICE ON MODERATION IN THE FRENCH REVOLUTION*

Through Lafayette and other social contacts, Jefferson knew a number of the men who led the French Revolution in its early period. Some met at his dinner table, where he privately discoursed on the need for moderate reforms, instead of violent revolution, rightly assuming that the French, after centuries of absolute monarchical rule, were not ready for self-government.

↑   ↑   ↑

I was much acquainted with the leading patriots of the [*National*] Assembly. Being from a country which had successfully passed through a similar reformation, they were disposed to my acquaintance, and had some confidence in me. I urged most strenuously an immediate compromise; to secure what the government was now ready to yield, and trust to future occasions for what might still be wanting. It was well understood that the King would grant at this time: 1. Freedom of person by habeas corpus. 2. Freedom of conscience. 3. Freedom of the press. 4. Trial by jury. 5. A representative legislature. 6. Annual meetings. 7. The origination of laws. 8. The exclusive right of taxation and appropriation. And 9. The responsibility of ministers; and with the exercise of these powers they would obtain in future whatever might be further necessary to improve and preserve their constitution. They thought otherwise, however, and events have proved their lamentable error. For after 30 years of war, foreign and domestic, the loss of millions of lives, the

* *Autobiography* (1821), pp. 129-130.

prostration of private happiness, and foreign subjugation of their own country for a time, they have obtained no more, nor even that securely.

— Reading No. 8 —

DEFENSE OF SHAYS' REBELLION

In 1786, Captain Daniel Shays, a destitute Massachusetts farmer, led an uprising by debt-ridden farmers whose grievances were unheeded by the state legislature. Shays' insurgents were militarily defeated at Petersham in February 1787. But the rebellion, although crushed, in the end did achieve its main objectives: direct taxes were not imposed in 1787, court fees were lowered, personal goods were exempted from being seized for debt. In this sense, the uprising bore out Jefferson's defense of it.

✟   ✟   ✟

A.*

I am persuaded myself that the good sense of the people will always be found to be the best army. They may be led astray for a moment, but will soon correct themselves. The people are the only censors of their governors: and even their errors will tend to keep these to the true principles of their institution. To punish these errors too severely would be to suppress the only safe guard of the public liberty. The way to prevent these irregular interpositions of the people [Shays' Rebellion] is to give them full information of their affairs through the channel of the public papers, and to contrive that those papers should penetrate the whole mass of the people. The basis of our governments being the opinion of the people, the very first object should be to keep that right and were it left to me to decide whether we should have

* Letter to Edward Carrington, January 16, 1787. Published in P. L. Ford, ed., *The Writings of Thomas Jefferson* IV (1894), pp. 359-360; also in S. K. Padover, ed. *A Jefferson Profile* (1956), pp. 44-45.

a government without newspapers or newspapers without a government, I should not hesitate a moment to prefer the latter. But I should mean that every man should receive those papers and be capable of reading them. I am convinced that those societies (as the Indians) which live without government enjoy in their general mass an infinitely greater degree of happiness than those who live under the European governments. Among the former, public opinion is in the place of law, and restrains morals as powerfully as laws ever did anywhere. Among the latter, under pretence of governing they have divided their nations into two classes, wolves and sheep. I do not exaggerate. This is a true picture of Europe. Cherish therefore the spirit of our people, and keep alive their attention. Do not be too severe on their errors, but reclaim them by enlightening them. If once they become inattentive to the public affairs, you and I, and Congress and Assemblies, judges and governors shall all become wolves. It seems to be the law of our general nature, in spite of individual exceptions; and experience declares that man is the only animal which devours his own kind, for I can apply no milder term to the governments of Europe, and to the general prey of the rich on the poor. . . .

B.*

. . . Those characters wherein fear predominates over hope may apprehend too much from these instances of irregularity [*Shays' Rebellion*]. They may conclude too hastily that nature has formed man insusceptible of any other government but that of force, a conclusion not founded in truth, nor experience. Societies exist under three forms sufficiently distinguishable. 1. Without government, as among our Indians. 2. Under governments wherein the will of every one has a just influence, as is the case in England in a slight degree, and in our states, in a great one. 3. Under governments of force: as is the case in all other monarchies and in most of the other republics. To have an idea of the curse of existence under

* Letter to James Madison, January 30, 1787. Published in P. L. Ford, ed., *The Writings of Thomas Jefferson,* IV (1894), pp. 361-363; also in S. K. Padover, *The World of the Founding Fathers* (1960), pp. 280-281.

these last, they must be seen. It is a government of wolves over sheep. It is a problem, not clear in my mind, that the 1st condition is not the best. But I believe it to be inconsistent with any great degree of population. The second state has a great deal of good in it. The mass of mankind under that enjoys a precious degree of liberty & happiness. It has its evils too: the principal of which is the turbulence to which it is subject. But weigh this against the oppressions of monarchy, and it becomes nothing. *Malo periculosam libertatem quam quietam servitutem.* Even this evil is productive of good. It prevents the degeneracy of government, and nourishes a general attention to the public affairs. I hold it that a little rebellion now and then is a good thing, & as necessary in the political world as storms in the physical. Unsuccessful rebellions indeed generally establish the encroachments on the rights of the people which have produced them. An observation of this truth should render honest republican governors so mild in their punishment of rebellions, as not to discourage them too much. It is a medicine necessary for the sound health of government.

C.*

God forbid we should ever be 20 years without such a rebellion. The people cannot be all, & always, well informed. The part which is wrong will be discontented in proportion to the importance of the facts they misconceive. If they remain quiet under such misconceptions it is a lethargy, the forerunner of death to the public liberty. We have had 13 States independent 11 years. There has been one rebellion. That comes to one rebellion in a century & a half for each State. What country before ever existed a century and a half without a rebellion? And what country can preserve its liberties if their rulers are not warned from time to time that their people preserve the spirit of resistance? Let them take arms. The remedy is to set them right as to facts, pardon & pacify them. What signify a few lives lost in a century or two? The tree of

---

* Letter to William Stephens Smith, November 13, 1787. Published in P. L. Ford, ed., *The Writings of Thomas Jefferson*, IV (1894), p. 467.

liberty must be refreshed from time to time with the blood of patriots & tyrants. It is its natural manure.

D.*

. . . The late rebellion in Massachusetts has given more alarm than I think it should have done. Calculate that one rebellion in 13 states in the course of 11 years, is but one for each state in a century and a half. No country should be so long without one. Nor will any degree of power in the hands of government prevent insurrections. France, with all its despotism, and two or three hundred thousand men always in arms has had three insurrections in the three years I have been here. . . . In Turkey, which Montesquieu supposes more despotic, insurrections are the events of every day. In England, where the hand of power is lighter than here [*France*], but heavier than with us they happen every half dozen years. Compare again the order, the moderation and the almost self extinguishment of ours. After all, it is my principle that the will of the majority should always prevail. . . . Above all things I hope the education of the common people will be attended to; convinced that on their good sense we may rely with the most security for the preservation of a due degree of liberty. . . .

* Letter to James Madison, December 20, 1787. Published in P. L. Ford, ed., *The Writings of Thomas Jefferson,* IV (1894), pp. 479-480.

— Reading No. 9 —

DEFENSE OF THE FRENCH REVOLUTION

Jefferson defended the French Revolution on two main grounds. One was that it would encourage the spread of liberty in Europe and the rest of the world; the other was that its success would strengthen, just as its failure might undermine, the American republic—in that day the only other republic of any importance in the world. Even the Reign of Terror and the execution of Louis XVI did not deflect him from viewing the French Revolution in larger historic perspective.

✒   ✒   ✒

A.*

The French Revolution proceeds steadily. . . . The success of that will ensure the progress of liberty in Europe, and its preservation here. The failure of that would have been a powerful argument with those who wish to introduce a king, lords and commons here. . . .

B.†

I still hope the French Revolution will issue happily. I feel that the permanence of our own leans in some

* Letter to Edmund Pendleton, July 24, 1791. Published in P. L. Ford, ed., *The Writings of Thomas Jefferson*, V (1895), p. 358.
† Letter to Edward Rutledge, August 29, 1791. Published in P. L. Ford, ed., *The Writings of Thomas Jefferson*, V (1895), p. 377.

degree on that, and that a failure there would be a powerful argument to prove that there must be a failure here.

C.*

The tone of your letters had for some time given me pain, on account of the extreme warmth with which they censured the proceedings of the Jacobins of France. I considered that sect as the same with the Republican patriots. . . . The Jacobins . . . tried the experiment of retaining their hereditary Executive. The experiment failed completely, and would have brought on the reestablishment of despotism had it been pursued. The Jacobins saw this, and that the expunging that officer [*Louis XVI*] was of absolute necessity. . . . In the struggle which was necessary, many guilty persons fell without the forms of trial, and with them some innocent. These I deplore as much as any body, & shall deplore some of them to the day of my death. But I deplore them as I should have done had they fallen in battle. It was necessary to use the arm of the people, a machine not quite so blind as balls and bombs, but blind to a certain degree. A few of their cordial friends met at their hands the fate of enemies. But time and truth will rescue & embalm their memories, while their posterity will be enjoying that very liberty for which they would never have hesitated to offer up their lives. The liberty of the whole earth was depending on the issue of the contest, and was ever such a prize won with so little innocent blood? My own affections have been deeply wounded by some of the martyrs to this cause, but rather than it should have failed, I would have seen half the earth desolated. Were there but an Adam & an Eve left in every country, & left free, it would be better than as it now is.

* Letter to William Short (Jefferson's former secretary in
   Paris), January 3, 1793. Published in P. L. Ford, ed.,
   The Writings of Thomas Jefferson, VI (1895), pp. 153-
   154; also in S. K. Padover, ed. *A Jefferson Profile* (1956),
   pp. 92-93.

— Reading No. 10 —

NEED FOR A BILL OF RIGHTS

After the Federal Constitution was made public (September 19, 1787), James Madison, one of its chief architects, sent a copy of it to his friend Jefferson in Paris. Jefferson, studying it carefully, was pleased with it in general, but felt it was incomplete without a Bill of Rights. In letters to Madison and other friends in America, he explained the need for a Bill of Rights as a guarantor of liberty. Madison undertook the successful task of championing such a Bill, which, as the first Ten Amendments to the Constitution, came into effect on December 15, 1791.

✔   ✔   ✔

A.*

I will . . . [*add*] a few words on the Constitution. . . . I like much the general idea of framing a government which should go on of itself peaceably, without need of continued recurrence to the State legislatures. I like the organization of the government into Legislative, Judiciary and Executive. I like the power given the Legislature to levy taxes. . . . I am captivated by the opposite claims of the great & little States, of the latter to equal, and the former to proportional influence. I am much pleased too with the substitution of the method of voting by persons, instead of that of voting by States; and I like the negative [*veto*] given to the Executive with a third of either House, though I should have liked it better had the Judiciary

---

* Letter to James Madison, December 20, 1787. Published in P. L. Ford, ed., *The Writings of Thomas Jefferson*, IV (1894), pp. 475-477; also in S. K. Padover, ed., *A Jefferson Profile* (1956), pp. 56-58.

been associated for that purpose, or invested with a similar and separate power. There are other good things of less moment.

I will now add what I do not like. First the omission of a Bill of Rights providing clearly & without the aid of sophisms for freedom of religion, freedom of the press, protection against standing armies, restriction against monopolies, the eternal & unremitting force of the habeas corpus laws, and trials by jury in all matters of fact triable by the laws of the land & not by the law of nations. . . . It was a hard conclusion to say because there has been no uniformity among the States as to the cases triable by jury, because some have been so incautious as to abandon this mode of trial, therefore the more prudent States shall be reduced to the same level of calamity. It would have been much more just & wise to have concluded the other way that as most of the States had judiciously preserved this palladium, those who had wandered should be brought back to it, and to have established a general right instead of a general wrong. Let me add that a Bill of Rights is what the people are entitled to against every government on earth, general or particular, & what no just government should refuse, or rest on inferences. . . .

B.*

There is a great deal of good in it [*Constitution*]. There are two things however which I dislike strongly. 1. The want of a declaration of rights. . . . 2. The perpetual re-eligibility of the President. This I fear will make an office for life first, & then hereditary. I was much an enemy of monarchy before I came to Europe. I am ten thousand times more so since I have seen what they are. There is scarcely an evil known in these countries which may not be traced to their king as its source, nor a good which is not derived from the small fibres of republicanism existing among them. I can further say with safety there is not a crowned head in Europe whose talents or merit would entitle him to be elected a vestryman by the people of any parish in America.

* Letter to George Washington, May 2, 1788. Published in P. L. Ford, ed., *The Writings of Thomas Jefferson*, V (1895), p. 8.

C.*

I sincerely rejoice at the acceptance of our new constitution by nine states.† It is a good canvass, on which some strokes only want retouching. What these are, I think are sufficiently manifested by the general voice from North to South, which calls for a Bill of Rights. It seems pretty generally understood that this should go to Juries, Habeas corpus, Standing armies, Printing, Religion and Monopolies. I conceive there may be difficulty in finding general modifications of these, suited to . . . all the states. But if such cannot be found then it is better to establish trials by Jury, the right of Habeas corpus, freedom of press and freedom of religion, in all cases, and to abolish standing armies in time of peace, and Monopolies in all cases, than not do it in any. The few cases wherein these things may do evil, cannot be weighed against the multitude wherein the want of them will do evil. In disputes between a foreigner and a native, a trial by jury may be improper. But if this exception cannot be agreed to, the remedy will be to model the jury giving the *mediatas linguae* in civil as well as criminal cases. Why suspend the Habeas corpus in insurrections and rebellions? The parties who may be arrested may be charged instantly with a well defined crime, of course the judge will remand them. If public safety requires that the government should have a man imprisoned on less probable testimony in those than in other emergencies, let him be taken and tried, retaken and retried, while the necessity continues, only giving him redress against the government for damages. Examine the history of England. See how few of the cases of the suspension of the Habeas corpus law have been worthy of that suspension. They have been either real treason wherein the parties might as well have been charged at once, or sham plots where it was shameful they should ever have been suspected. . . . I hope therefore a Bill of Rights will be formed to guard

---

* Letter to James Madison, July 31, 1788. Published in P. L. Ford, ed., *The Writings of Thomas Jefferson*, V (1895), pp. 45-47.
† New Hampshire was the ninth state to ratify the Constitution, on June 21, 1788.

the people against the federal government, as they are
already guarded against their state governments in most
instances.

D.*

Experience proves [*critics say*] the inefficacy of a Bill
of Rights. True. But though it is not absolutely efficacious
under all circumstances, it is of great potency always, and
rarely inefficacious. A brace the more will often keep up
the building which would have fallen with that brace the
less. There is a remarkable difference between the characters of the inconveniences which attend a declaration
of rights, & those which attend the want of it. The inconveniences of the declaration are that it may cramp
government in its useful exertions. But the evil of this is
short-lived, trivial & reparable. The inconveniences of the
want of a Declaration are permanent, afflicting & ir-
reparable. They are in constant progression from bad to
worse. The executive in our governments is not the sole,
it is scarcely the principal object of my jealousy. The
tyranny of the legislatures is the most formidable dread
at present, and will be for long years. That of the executive will come in its turn, but it will be at a remote
period. I know there are some among us who would now
establish a monarchy. But they are inconsiderable in number and weight of character. The rising race are all republicans. We were educated in royalism; no wonder if
some of us retain that idolatry still. Our young people
are educated in republicanism, an apostasy from that to
royalism is unprecedented & impossible. I am much
pleased with the prospect that a declaration of rights will
be added; and hope it will be done in that way which will
not endanger the whole frame of the government, or any
essential part of it.

* Letter to James Madison, March 15, 1789. Published in
   P. L. Ford, ed., *The Writings of Thomas Jefferson,* V
   (1895), pp. 82-83; also in S. K. Padover, ed., *The Complete Jefferson* (1943), pp. 124-125.

E.*

The operations which have taken place in America lately [*the Philadelphia Constitutional Convention of 1787 and the subsequent State ratification conventions*], fill me with pleasure. . . . The example of changing a constitution by assembling the wise men of the State, instead of assembling armies, will be worth as much to the world as the former examples we had given them. The constitution too which was the result of our deliberations, is unquestionably the wisest ever yet presented to men. . . . It has some defects. I am one of those who think it a defect that the important rights, not placed in security by the frame of the constitution itself were not explicitly secured by a supplementary declaration. There are rights which it is useless to surrender to the government, and which governments have yet always been found to invade. These are the rights of thinking, and publishing our thoughts by speaking or writing; the right of free commerce; the right of personal freedom. There are instruments for administering the government, so peculiarly trustworthy, that we should never leave the legislature at liberty to change them. The new constitution has secured these in the executive and legislative departments; but not in the judiciary. It should have established trials by the people themselves, that is to say by jury. There are instruments so dangerous to the rights of the nation, and which place them so totally at the mercy of their governors, that those governors, whether legislative or executive, should be restrained from keeping such instruments on foot, but in well-defined cases. Such an instrument is a standing army. . . . A declaration of rights, as a supplement to the constitution where that is silent, is wanting to secure us in these points. . . .

* Letter to David Humphreys, March 18, 1789. Published in P. L. Ford, ed., *The Writings of Thomas Jefferson*, V (1895), pp. 89-90; also S. K. Padover, ed., *A Jefferson Profile* (1956), pp. 74-75.

— Reading No. 11 —

HAMILTON'S MEDDLING AND CORRUPT PRACTICES*

The struggle between Jefferson and Hamilton was reflected in the press. Anti-Jeffersonian charges were made in John Fenno's pro-Hamilton Gazette of the United States *and countered in Benjamin Franklin Bache's pro-Jeffersonian* General Advertiser (later Aurora). *Concerned that the clash would have an adverse effect on the country, President Washington appealed to both members of his Cabinet for conciliation. In the selection below, Jefferson, defending his position, accuses Hamilton of meddling and of corrupting the legislature with his financial policies.*

✓   ✓   ✓

When I embarked in the government, it was with a determination to intermeddle not at all with the legislature, & as little as possible with my co-departments. The first and only instance of variance from the former part of my resolution, I was duped into by the Secretary of the Treasury and made a tool of forwarding his schemes, not then sufficiently understood by me; and of all the errors of my political life, this has occasioned me the deepest regret. . . .

That I have utterly, in my private conversations, disapproved of the system of the Secretary of the Treasury, I acknowledge & avow; and this was not merely a speculative difference. His system flowed from principles ad-

* Letter to George Washington, September 9, 1792. Published in P. L. Ford, ed., *The Writings of Thomas Jefferson,* VI (1895), pp. 102-104.

verse to liberty, & was calculated to undermine and de-
molish the republic, by creating an influence of his department over the members of the legislature. I saw this
influence actually produced, & its first fruits to be the
establishment of the great outlines of his project by the
votes of the very persons who, having swallowed his bait
were laying themselves out to profit by his plans. . . .
These were no longer the votes then of the representatives
of the people, but of deserters from the rights & interests
of the people; & it was impossible to consider their decisions, which had nothing in view but to enrich themselves,
as the measures of the fair majority, which ought always
to be respected. . . . So that if the question be By whose
fault is it that Colo. Hamilton & myself have not drawn
together? The answer will depend on that to two other
questions; whose principles of administration best justify,
by their purity, conscientious adherence? And which of us
has, notwithstanding, stepped farthest into the control of
the department of the other?

— Reading No. 12 —

CONDITION OF THE ENGLISH POOR*

A comparison of the conditions of Great Britain and the United States . . . would be an interesting subject indeed. . . . I will give you . . . the result of my reflections on the subject. . . . The population of England is composed of three descriptions of persons. . . . These are: 1. The aristocracy, comprehending the nobility, the wealthy commoners, the high grades of priesthood, and the officers of government. 2. The laboring class. 3. The eleemosynary class, or paupers, who are about one-fifth of the whole. The aristocracy, which have the laws and government in their hands, have so managed them as to reduce the third description below the means of supporting life, even by labor; and to force the second, whether employed in agriculture or the arts, to the maximum of labor which the construction of the human body can endure, and to the minimum of food, and of the meanest kind, which will preserve it in life, and in strength sufficient to perform its functions. To obtain food enough, and clothing, not only their whole strength must be unremittingly exerted, but the utmost dexterity also which they can acquire. . . . The less dexterous individuals, falling into the eleemosynary ranks, furnish materials for armies and navies to defend their country. . . . A society thus constituted possesses certainly the means of defence. But what does it defend? The pauperism of the lowest class, the abject oppression of the laboring, and the luxury,

* Letter to Dr. Thomas Cooper, September 10, 1814. Published in A. A. Lipscomb, ed., *The Writings of Thomas Jefferson,* XIV (1904), pp. 180-184.

the riot, the domination and the vicious happiness of the aristocracy. In their hands, the paupers are used as tools to maintain their own wretchedness, and to keep down the laboring portion by shooting them whenever the desperation produced by the cravings of their stomachs drives them into riots. Such is the happiness of scientific England; now let us see the American side of the medal.

And, first, we have no paupers, the old and crippled among us, who possess nothing and have no families to take care of them, being too few to merit notice as a separate section of society, or to affect a general estimate. The great mass of our population is of laborers; our rich, who can live without labor, either manual or professional, being few, and of moderate wealth. Most of the laboring class possess property, cultivate their own lands, have families, and from the demand for their labor are enabled to exact from the rich and the competent such prices as enable them to be fed abundantly, clothed above mere decency, to labor moderately and raise their families. They are not driven to the ultimate resources of dexterity and skill, because their wares will sell. . . .

The wealthy, on the other hand, and those at their ease, know nothing of what the Europeans call luxury. They have only somewhat more of the comforts and decencies of life than those who furnish them. Can any condition of society be more desirable than this?

— Reading No. 13 —

THE SUPERIORITY OF FARMERS

A.*

Those who labor in the earth are the chosen people of God, if ever he had a chosen people, whose breasts he has made his peculiar deposit for substantial and genuine virtue. It is the focus in which He keeps alive that sacred fire, which otherwise might escape from the face of the earth. Corruption of morals in the mass of cultivators is a phenomenon of which no age nor nation has furnished an example. It is the mark set on those, who not looking up to heaven, to their own soil and industry, as does the husbandman, for their subsistence, depend for it on casualties and caprice of customers. Dependence begets subservience and venality, suffocates the germ of virtue, and prepares fit tools for the designs of ambition. . . . Generally speaking the proportion which the aggregate of the other classes of citizens bears in any state to that of its husbandmen, is the proportion of its unsound to its healthy parts. . . .

B.†

Cultivators of the earth are the most valuable citizens. They are the most vigorous, the most independent, the most virtuous, & they are tied to their country & wedded to its liberty & interests by the most lasting bonds. As long, therefore, as they can find employment in this line, I would not convert them into mariners, artisans or anything else.

* *Notes on Virginia* (1782), Query XIX.
† Letter to John Jay, August 23, 1785. Published in P. L. Ford, ed., *The Writings of Thomas Jefferson,* IV (1894), p. 88.

SHIPPING AND WAR

A.*

Never was so much false arithmetic employed on any subject, as that which has been employed to persuade nations that it is their interest to go to war. Were the money which it has cost to gain, at the close of a long war, a little town, or a little territory, the right to cut wood here, or to catch fish there, expended in improving what they already possess, in making roads, opening rivers, building ports, improving the arts, and finding employment for their idle poor, it would render them much stronger, much wealthier and happier. This I hope will be our wisdom. And perhaps, to remove as much as possible the occasions of making war, it might be better for us to abandon the ocean altogether, that being the element whereon we shall be principally exposed to jostle with other nations: to leave to others to bring what we shall want, and to carry what we can spare. This would make us invulnerable to Europe, by offering none of our property to their prize, and would turn all our citizens to the cultivation of the earth; and, I repeat it again, cultivators of the earth are the most virtuous and independent citizens. It might be time enough to seek employment for them at sea, when the land no longer offers it.

B.†

Cultivators of the earth are the most valuable citizens. . . . As long, therefore, as they can find employment in

* *Notes on Virginia* (1782), Query XXII.
† Letter to John Jay, August 23, 1785. Published in P. L. Ford, ed., *The Writings of Thomas Jefferson,* IV (1894), pp. 88-90.

this line, I would not convert them into mariners, artisans or anything else. . . . This is not the case as yet, & probably will not be for a considerable time. . . . However we are not free to decide this question on principles of theory only. Our people are decided in the opinion that it is necessary for us to take a share in the occupation of the ocean, & their established habits induce them to require that the sea be kept open to them. . . . I think it a duty in those entrusted with the administration of their affairs to conform themselves to the decided choice of their constituents: and that, therefore, we should in every instance preserve an equality of right to them in the transportation of commodities, in the right of fishing, & in the other uses of the sea.

But what will be the consequence? Frequent wars without a doubt. Their property will be violated on the sea, & in foreign ports, their persons will be insulted, imprisoned, etc. for pretended debts, contracts, crimes, contraband, etc. These insults must be resented, even if we had no feelings, yet to prevent their eternal repetition, or in other words, our commerce on the ocean & in other countries must be paid for by frequent war. The justest dispositions in ourselves will not secure us against it. . . . This reasoning leads to the necessity of some naval force. . . . If a war with England should take place, it seems to me that the first thing necessary would be a resolution to abandon the carrying trade because we cannot protect it. Foreign nations must in that case be invited to bring us what we want & to take our productions in their own bottoms. . . . Indeed I look forward with horror to the very possible case of war with an European power, & think there is no protection against them but from the possession of some force on the sea.

CHANGE OF MIND IN FAVOR OF MANUFACTURING*

In the letter given below, written to a prominent Boston merchant and friendly political leader, Jefferson explains his change of mind in regard to manufacturing. A quarter century of wars, during which period both the British and the French so harassed American shipping that they virtually excluded it from the oceans, made it necessary, Jefferson concluded, to replace badly needed imports with domestic production.

✓   ✓   ✓

You tell me I am quoted by those who wish to continue our dependence on England for manufactures. There was a time when I might have been so quoted with more candor, but within the thirty years which have since elapsed, how are circumstances changed! . . .

We have experienced what we did not then believe, that there exists both profligacy and power enough to exclude us from the field of interchange with other nations: that to be independent for the comforts of life we must fabricate them ourselves. We must now place the manufacturer by the side of the agriculturist. The former question . . . assumes a new form. Shall we make our own comforts, or go without them, at the will of a foreign nation? He, therefore, who is now against domestic manufacture, must be for reducing us either to dependence on that foreign nation, or to be clothed in skins, and to live like wild beasts in dens and caverns. I am not one of these; experience has taught me that manufactures are now as necessary to our independence as to our comfort.

* Letter to Benjamin Austin, January 9, 1816. Published in P. L. Ford, ed., *The Writings of Thomas Jefferson*, X (1899), pp. 8-10.

— Reading No. 16 —

THE KENTUCKY RESOLUTIONS*

I. Resolved, That the several States composing the United States of America, are not united on the principle of unlimited submission to their general government; but that, by a compact under the . . . Constitution for the United States . . . , they constituted a general government for special purposes—delegated to that government certain definite powers, reserving each State to itself, the residuary mass of right to their own self-government. . . .

II. Resolved, That . . . the act of Congress [*Sedition Act*] . . . , and all their other acts which assume to create, define, or punish crimes, other than those so enumerated in the Constitution, are altogether void, and of no force. . . .

III. Resolved, That . . . no power over the freedom of religion, freedom of speech, or freedom of the press being delegated to the United States by the Constitution . . . , all lawful powers respecting the same did of right remain, and were reserved to the States. . . .

VIII. Resolved, That . . . to take from the States all the powers of self-government and transfer them to a general and consolidated government, without regard to the special delegations and reservations solemnly agreed to in that compact [*Federal Constitution*], is not for the peace, happiness or prosperity of these States; . . . that every State has a natural right in cases not within the compact . . . , to nullify of their own authority all assumptions of power by others. . . .

* *The Kentucky Resolutions*, printed by the Kentucky Legislature, November 10, 1798. Published in P. L. Ford, ed., *The Writings of Thomas Jefferson*, VII (1896), pp. 289-308.

— Reading No. 17 —

"THIS SIMPLE AND ECONOMICAL MODE OF GOVERNMENT"

A.

Decentralization and Liberty*

Our country is too large to have all its affairs directed by a single government. Public servants at such a distance, & from under the eye of their constituents, must, from the circumstance of distance, be unable to administer & overlook all the details necessary for the good government of the citizens, and the same circumstance, by rendering detection impossible to their constituents, will invite the public agents to corruption, plunder & waste. And I do verily believe, that if the principle were to prevail, of a common law being in force in the U. S. (which principle possesses the general government at once of all the powers of the state governments, and reduces us to a single consolidated government), it would become the most corrupt government on the earth. . . . What an augmentation of the field for jobbing, speculating, plundering, office-building & office-hunting would be produced by an assumption of all the state powers into the hands of the general government. The true theory of our Constitution is surely the wisest & best, that the states are independent as to everything within themselves, & united as to everything respecting foreign nations. Let the general government be reduced to foreign concerns only,

* Letter to Gideon Granger (appointed by Jefferson Postmaster General in 1801), August 13, 1800. Published in P. L. Ford, ed., *The Writings of Thomas Jefferson*, VII (1896), pp. 451-452.

and let our affairs be disentangled from those of all other nations, except as to commerce, which the merchants will manage the better, the more they are left free to manage for themselves, and our general government may be reduced to a very simple organization, & a very unexpensive one; a few plain duties to be performed by a few servants.

B.

State Governments—Barriers of Our Liberty*

But the true barriers of our liberty in this country are our State governments; and the wisest conservative power ever contrived by man, is that of which our Revolution and present government found us possessed. Seventeen† distinct States, amalgamated into one as to their foreign concerns, but single and independent as to their internal administration, regularly organized with legislature and governor resting on the choice of the people, and enlightened by a free press, can never be so fascinated by the arts of one man, as to submit voluntarily to his usurpation. Nor can they be constrained to it by any force he can possess. While that may paralyze the single State in which it happens to be encamped, sixteen others, spread over a country of two thousand miles diameter, rise up on every side, ready organized for deliberation by a constitutional legislature, and for action by their governor, constitutionally the commander of the militia of the State, that is to say, of every man in it able to bear arms. . . . The republican government of France was lost without a struggle, because the part of 'un et indivisible' had prevailed; no provincial organizations existed to which the people might rally under authority of the laws. . . .

* Letter to A. C. V. C. Destutt de Tracy, January 26, 1811. Published in P. L. Ford, ed., *The Writings of Thomas Jefferson,* IX (1898), pp. 308-310.
† By this time, the 13 original States had been joined by four more: Vermont (1791), Kentucky (1792), Tennessee (1796), and Ohio (1803).

— Reading No. 18 —

JEFFERSON'S POLITICAL CREDO*

In confutation of . . . calumnies . . . , I shall make to you a profession of my political faith; in confidence that you will consider every imputation on me of a contrary complexion, as . . . falsehood and calumny.

I do then, with sincere zeal, wish an inviolable preservation of our present federal constitution, according to the true sense in which it was adopted by the States . . . ; and I am opposed to the monarchising its features by the forms of its administration, with a view to conciliate a first transition to a President and Senate for life, and from that to a hereditary tenure of these offices, and thus to worm out the elective principle. I am for preserving to the States the powers not yielded by them to the Union, and to the legislature of the Union its constitutional share in the division of powers; and I am not for transferring all the powers of the States to the general government, and all those of that government to the Executive branch. I am for a government rigorously frugal and simple, applying all the possible savings of the public revenue to the discharge of the national debt; and not for a multiplication of officers and salaries merely to make partisans, and for increasing, by every device, the public debt, on the principle of its being a public blessing. I am for relying, for internal defence, on our militia solely, till actual invasion, and for such a naval force only as may protect our coasts and harbors from such depredations as we have experienced; and not for a standing army in time of peace, which may overawe the public sentiment; nor for a navy,

* Letter to Elbridge Gerry, January 26, 1799. Published in P. L. Ford, ed., *The Writings of Thomas Jefferson*, VII (1896), pp. 327-329.

which, by its own expenses and the eternal wars in which it will implicate us, will grind us with public burthens, and sink us under them. I am for free commerce with all nations; political connection with none; and little or no diplomatic establishment. And I am not for linking ourselves by new treaties with the quarrels of Europe; entering that field of slaughter to preserve their balance, or joining in the confederacy of kings to war against the principles of liberty. I am for freedom of religion, and against all maneuvres to bring about a legal ascendancy of one sect over another; for freedom of the press, and against all violations of the constitution to silence by force and not by reason the complaints of criticisms, just or unjust, of our citizens against the conduct of their agents. And I am for encouraging the progress of science in all its branches; and not for raising a hue and cry against the sacred name of philosophy. . . . The first object of my heart is my own country. In that is embarked my family, my fortune, and my own existence. I have not one farthing of interest, nor one fibre of attachment out of it, nor a single motive of preference of any one nation to another, but in proportion as they are more or less friendly to us. . . .

These, my friend, are my principles; they are unquestionably the principles of the great body of our fellow citizens. . . .

— Reading No. 19 —

AMERICAN REPUBLICANISM AS A WORLD IDEAL

A. *

A just and solid republican government maintained here, will be a standing monument & example for the aim & imitation of the people of other countries; and I join with you in the hope and belief that they will see, from our example, that a free government is of all others the most energetic; that . . . our revolution & its consequences will ameliorate the condition of man over a great portion of the globe. . . . The leaders on the other side . . . have endeavored to render philosophy and republicanism terms of reproach, to persuade us that man cannot be governed but by the rod. I shall have the happiness of living & dying in the contrary hope.

B. †

Our people in a body are wise, because they are under the unrestrained and unperverted operation of their own understandings. . . . A nation, composed of such materials, and free . . . from distressing wants, furnishes hopeful implements for the interesting experiment of self-government; and we feel that we are acting under obligations not confined to the limits of our own society. It is

---

* Letter to John Dickinson, March 6, 1801. Published in **P. L. Ford**, ed., *The Writings of Thomas Jefferson,* VIII (1897), p. 8.
† Letter to Joseph Priestley, June 19, 1802. Published in **P. L. Ford**, ed., *The Writings of Thomas Jefferson,* VIII (1897), pp. 158-159.

impossible not to be sensible that we are acting for all mankind; that circumstances denied to others, but indulged to us, have imposed on us the duty of proving what is the degree of freedom and self-government in which a society may venture to leave its individual members.

— Reading No. 20 —

PARTISAN BITTERNESS IN JEFFERSON'S DAY*

Observers of the American scene in the early years of the Republic were struck by the violence of party feelings. The selection below is from a book by a French traveler who, among other places, also visited Jefferson's Monticello in 1796.

ꜰ   ꜰ   ꜰ

But the spirit of party is carried to excess in America; men who embrace the opinion of Mr. Jefferson, attack their opponents with imputations, no doubt, equally unfounded. In all party-proceedings neither reason nor justice can be expected from either side, and very seldom strict morality with respect to the means employed to serve the favourite cause; one cause alone appears good, everything besides is deemed bad, nay criminal. . . Personal resentments assume the colour of public spirit and . . . the most atrocious calumnies spread. . . .

* Duke de la Rochefoucauld-Liancourt, *Travels Through the United States . . . , in the Years 1795, 1796, and 1797* (London, 2d ed., 1800), Vol. III.

JEFFERSON'S FIRST INAUGURAL ADDRESS*

A.

General Principles

. . . All, too, will bear in mind this sacred principle, that though the will of the majority is in all cases to prevail, that will to be rightful must be reasonable; that the minority possesses their equal rights, which equal law must protect. . . . Let us, then, fellow-citizens, unite with one heart and one mind. Let us restore to social intercourse that harmony and affection without which liberty and even life itself are but dreary things. And let us reflect that, having banished from our land that religious intolerance under which mankind so long bled and suffered, we have yet gained little if we countenance a political intolerance as despotic, as wicked, and capable of as bitter and bloody persecutions. . . . But every difference of opinion is not a difference of principle. We have called by different names brethren of the same principle. We are all Republicans, we are all Federalists. If there be any among us who would wish to dissolve this Union or to change its republican form, let them stand undisturbed as monuments of the safety with which error of opinion may be tolerated where reason is left free to combat it. I

---

* Delivered at Washington, D. C., March 4, 1801. Published in J. D. Richardson, ed., *A Compilation of the Messages and Papers of the Presidents*, I (1899), pp. 321-324; also in *Inaugural Addresses of the Presidents of the United States* (82d Congr., 2d Sess., House Document No. 540: 1952), pp. 11-14; S. K. Padover, ed., *The Complete Jefferson* (1943), pp. 384-387.

know, indeed, that some honest men fear that a republican government can not be strong, that this Government is not strong enough; but would the honest patriot, in the full tide of successful experiment, abandon a government which has so far kept us free and firm on the theoretic and visionary fear that this Government, the world's best hope, may by possibility want energy to preserve itself? I trust not. I believe this, on the contrary, the strongest Government on earth. I believe it the only one where every man, at the call of the law, would fly to the standard of the law, and would meet invasions of the public order as his own personal concern. Sometimes it is said that man can not be trusted with the government of himself. Can he, then, be trusted with the government of others? Or have we found angels in the forms of kings to govern him? Let history answer this question.

Let us, then, with courage and confidence pursue our own Federal and Republican principles, our attachment to union and representative government. . . . Still one thing more, fellow-citizens—a wise and frugal Government, which shall restrain men from injuring one another, shall leave them otherwise free to regulate their own pursuits of industry and improvement, and shall not take from the mouth of labor the bread it has earned. This is the sum of good government, and this is necessary to close the circle of our felicities. . . .

B.

His Program

. . . It is proper you should understand what I deem the essential principles of our Government, and consequently those which ought to shape its Administration. I will compress them within the narrowest compass they will bear. . . . Equal and exact justice to all men, of whatever state or persuasion, religious or political; peace, commerce, and honest friendship with all nations, entangling alliances with none; the support of the State governments in all their rights, as the most competent administrations for our domestic concerns and the surest bulwarks against antirepublican tendencies; the preservation of the General Government in its whole constitutional vigor, as the sheet anchor of our peace at home and safety abroad; a jealous care of the right of election by the people—a mild and safe corrective of abuses which are lopped by the sword of revolution where peaceable remedies are unprovided; absolute acquiescence in the decisions of the majority, the vital principle of republics, from which there is no appeal but to force, the vital principle and immediate parent of despotism; a well-disciplined militia, our best reliance in peace and for the first moments of war, till regulars may relieve them; the supremacy of the civil over the military authority; economy in the public expense, that labor may be lightly burthened; the honest payment of our debts and sacred preservation of the public faith; encouragement of agriculture, and of commerce as its handmaid; the diffusion of information and arraignment of all abuses at the bar of the public reason; freedom of religion; freedom of the press, and freedom of person under the protection of the habeas corpus, and trial by juries impartially selected. These principles form the bright constellation which has gone before us and guided our steps through an age of revolution and reformation. The wisdom of our sages and blood of our heroes have been devoted to their attainment. They should be the creed of our political faith, the text of civic instruction, the touchstone by which to try the services of those we trust; and should we wander from them in moments of error or of alarm, let us hasten to retrace our steps and to regain the road which alone leads to peace, liberty, and safety. . . .

— Reading No. 22 —

EXAMPLE OF A FEDERALIST ATTACK ON JEFFERSON*

The general political tone of the time was violently polemical. The Federalists, if anything, tended towards more personal vituperation than the Republicans. Name-calling was a common political technique.† Henry Adams, the great-grandson of John Adams, in his History of the United States, I (1889), p. 80, thus described the image that the Federalists had of the Jeffersonians: "Every dissolute intriguer, loose-liver, forger, false-coiner, and prison-bird; every hare-brained, loud-talking demagogue; every speculator, scoffer, and atheist—was a follower of Jefferson; and Jefferson was himself the incarnation of their theories." The example given below is from Theodore Dwight, a leading Federalist and brother of the famous Yale President Timothy Dwight.

We have now reached the consummation of Democratic blessedness. We have a country governed by block-heads, and knaves; the ties of marriage, with all its felicities, are severed, and destroyed; our wives and our daughters are thrown into the stews; our children are cast into the world from the breast, and forgotten; filial piety is extinguished. . . . Can the imagination paint any thing more dreadful on this side hell? . . .

* T. Dwight, *Oration* (pamphlet: 1801).
† See S. K. Padover, *Jefferson* (1942), Ch. XII, for a description of the campaign of 1800.

— Reading No. 23 —

JEFFERSON'S CHARACTER
AND APPEARANCE*

The description given below is by Thomas Jefferson Randolph (1792-1875), Jefferson's favorite grandson and executor of his estate. Randolph, a prominent Virginia financier and political figure, was the first editor of his grandfather's papers, Memoir, Correspondence and Miscellanies, from the Papers of Thomas Jefferson, *4 volumes, 1829.*

✓   ✓   ✓

His manners were of that polished school of the Colonial Government, so remarkable in its day—under no circumstances violating any of those minor conventional observances which constitute the well-bred gentleman, courteous and considerate to all persons. On riding out with him, when a lad, we met a Negro who bowed to us; he returned his bow, I did not; turning to me he asked, 'Do you permit a Negro to be more of a gentleman than yourself?' . . .

Mr. Jefferson's hair, when young was of a reddish cast, sandy as he advanced in years—his eye, hazel—dying in his 84th year, he had not lost a tooth, or had one defective; his skin, thin, peeling from his face on exposure to the sun. . . . His countenance was mild and benignant, and attractive to strangers. . . . Mr. Jefferson's stature was commanding, six feet two and a half inches in height, well formed, indicating strength, activity, and robust health; his

---

* Thomas Jefferson Randolph, letter to Henry S. Randall;
    published in Randall's *The Life of Thomas Jefferson,* III
    (1857), Appendix No. XXXVI.

carriage, erect; step firm and elastic, which he preserved to his death; his temper, naturally strong, under perfect control—his courage, cool and impassive—no one ever knew him exhibit trepidation—his moral courage of the highest order—his will, firm and inflexible—it was remarked of him that he never abandoned a plan, a principle, or a friend. A bold and fearless rider, you saw at a glance, from his easy and confident seat, that he was master of his horse, which was usually the fine blood horse of Virginia. The only impatience of temper he ever exhibited, was with his horse, which he subdued to his will by a fearless application of the whip, on the slightest manifestation of restiveness.

— Reading No. 24 —

FREEDOM TO CRITICIZE*

. . . They [*the Federalists*] fill their newspapers with falsehoods, calumnies, and audacities. . . . We are going fairly through the experiment whether freedom of discussion, unaided by coercion, is not sufficient for the propagation and protection of truth, and for the maintenance of an administration pure and upright in its actions and views. No one ought to feel, under this experiment, more than myself. Nero wished all the necks of Rome united in one, that he might sever them at a blow. So our ex-Federalists, wishing to have a single representative of all the objects of their hatred, honor me with that post, and exhibit against me such atrocities as no nation had ever before heard or endured. I shall protect them in the right of lying and calumniating.

* Written to a friend in 1803. Published in S. K. Padover, *Jefferson* (1942), pp. 329-330.

TOLERANCE OF OPINION*

In stating prudential rules for our government in society, I must not omit the important one of never entering into dispute or argument with another. I never saw an instance of one of two disputants convincing the other by argument. I have seen many, on their getting warm, becoming rude, & shooting one another. Conviction is the effect of our own dispassionate reasoning, either in solitude, or weighing within ourselves, dispassionately, what we hear from others. . . . It was one of the rules which above all others, made Doctor Franklin the most amiable of men in society, 'never to contradict anybody.' If he was urged to announce an opinion, he did it rather by asking questions, as if for information, or by suggesting doubts.

When I hear another express an opinion which is not mine, I say to myself, he has a right to his opinion, as I to mine; why should I question it? His error does me no injury, and shall I become a Don Quixote, to bring all men by force of argument to one opinion? If a fact be misstated, it is probable he is gratified by a belief of it, & I have no right to deprive him of the gratification. If he wants information, he will ask it, & then I will give it in measured terms; but if he still believes his own story, & shows a desire to dispute the fact with me, I hear him & say nothing. It is his affair, not mine, if he prefers error.

* Letter to his grandson, Thomas Jefferson Randolph, November 24, 1808. Published in P. L. Ford, ed., *The Writings of Thomas Jefferson,* IX (1898), p. 232.

— Reading No. 26 —

FREEDOM OF EXPRESSION

A.

Freedom of the Press as an "Experiment" *

During this course of administration, and in order to disturb it, the artillery of the press has been levelled against us, charged with whatsoever its licentiousness could devise or dare. These abuses of an institution so important to freedom and science, are deeply to be regretted, inasmuch as they tend to lessen its usefulness, and to sap its safety; they might, indeed, have been corrected by the wholesome punishments reserved and provided by the laws of the several States against falsehood and defamation; but public duties more urgent press on the time of public servants, and the offenders have therefore been left to find their punishment in the public indignation.

Nor was it uninteresting to the world, that an experiment should be fairly and fully made, whether freedom of discussion, unaided by power, is not sufficient for the propagation and protection of truth—whether a government, conducting itself in the true spirit of its constitution, with zeal and purity, and doing no act which it would be unwilling the whole world should witness, can be written down by falsehood and defamation. The experiment has

* Second Inaugural Address, March 4, 1805. Published in J. D. Richardson, *A Compilation of the Messages and Papers of the Presidents*, I (1899), p. 381; also in *Inaugural Addresses of the Presidents of the United States* (82d Congr., 2d Sess. House Document No. 540: 1952), pp. 17-18; S. K. Padover, *The World of the Founding Fathers* (1960), pp. 278-279.

been tried; you have witnessed the scene; our fellow citizens have looked on, cool and collected; they saw the latent source from which these outrages proceeded; they gathered around their public functionaries, and when the constitution called them to the decision by suffrage, they pronounced their verdict, honorable to those who had served them, and consolatory to the friend of man, who believes he may be intrusted with his own affairs.

No inference is here intended, that the laws, provided by the State against false and defamatory publications, should not be enforced; he who has time, renders a service to public morals and public tranquillity, in reforming these abuses by the salutary coercions of the law; but the experiment is noted, to prove that, since truth and reason have maintained their ground against false opinions in league with false facts, the press, confined to truth, needs no other legal restraint; the public judgment will correct false reasonings and opinions, on a full hearing of all parties; and no other definite line can be drawn between the inestimable liberty of the press and its demoralizing licentiousness. If there be still improprieties which this rule would not restrain, its supplement must be sought in the censorship of public opinion.

B.

Favors Press Freedom, Despite Calumnies*

As to myself, conscious that there was not a *truth* on earth which I feared should be known, I have lent myself willingly as the subject of a great experiment, which was to prove that an administration, conducting itself with integrity and common understanding, cannot be battered down, even by the falsehoods of a licentious press, and consequently still less by the press, as restrained within the legal & wholesome limits of truth. This experiment was wanting for the world to demonstrate the falsehood of the pretext that freedom of the press is incompatible with orderly government. I have never therefore even contradicted the thousands of calum-

* Letter to Thomas Seymour, February 11, 1807. Published in P. L. Ford, ed., *The Writings of Thomas Jefferson*, IX (1898), p. 30.

nies so industriously propagated against myself. But the
fact being once established, that the press is impotent
when it abandons itself to falsehood, I leave to others to
restore it to its strength, by recalling it within the pale
of truth. Within that it is a noble institution, equally the
friend of science & of civil liberty.

C.

Opposes Prosecution for Libel*

I had no conception there were persons enough to
support a paper whose stomachs could bear such aliment
as the enclosed papers contain. They are far beyond even
the Washington Federalist. To punish however is im-
practicable until the body of the people, from whom
juries are to be taken, get their minds to rights; and even
then I doubt its expediency. While a full range is proper
for actions by individuals, either private or public, for
slanders affecting them, I would wish much to see the
experiment tried of getting along without public prosecutions for *libels*. I believe we can do it. Patience and well
doing, instead of punishment, if it can be found sufficiently efficacious, would be a happy change in the instruments of government.

D.

No Prosecution for Libel †

The Federalists having failed in destroying the freedom
of the press by their gag-law [*Sedition Act of 1798*], seem
to have attacked it in an opposite form, that is by pushing
its licentiousness & its lying to such a degree of prosti-
tution as to deprive it of all credit. And the fact is that
so abandoned are the tory presses in this particular that
even the least informed of the people have learnt that
nothing in a newspaper is to be believed. This is a danger-

* Letter to Attorney-General Levi Lincoln, March 24, 1802.
Published in P. L. Ford, ed., *The Writings of Thomas
Jefferson*, VIII (1897), p. 39.
† Letter to Thomas McKean (Governor of Pennsylvania),
February 19, 1803. Published in P. L. Ford, ed., *The
Writings of Thomas Jefferson*, VIII (1897), pp. 218-219.

ous state of things, and the press ought to be restored to its credibility if possible. The restraints provided by the laws of the states are sufficient for this if applied. And I have therefore long thought that a few prosecutions of the most prominent offenders would have a wholesome effect in restoring the integrity of the presses. Not a general prosecution, for that would look like persecution, but a selected one. The paper I now inclose appears to me to offer as good an instance in every respect to make an example of, as can be selected.

— Reading No. 27 —

NEWSPAPERS AS "AVENUES TO TRUTH"*

No experiment can be more interesting than that we are now trying, which we trust will end in establishing the fact that man may be governed by reason & truth. Our first object should therefore be to leave open to him all the avenues to truth. The most effectual hitherto found is the freedom of the press. It is therefore the first shut up by those who fear the investigation of their actions. The firmness with which the people have withstood the late abuses of the press, the discernment they have manifested between truth & falsehood shew that they may safely be trusted to hear everything true and false & to form a correct judgment between them.

* Letter to John Tyler, 1803. Published in S. K. Padover, *Jefferson* (1942), p. 330.

— Reading No. 28 —

THE PRESS AND PUBLIC OPINION

A.*

Indeed the abuses of the freedom of the press here have been carried to a length never before known or borne by any civilized nation. But it is so difficult to draw a clear line of separation between the abuse and the wholesome use of the press, that as yet we have found it better to trust the public judgment, rather than the magistrate, with the discrimination between truth and falsehood. And hitherto the public judgment has performed that office with wonderful correctness.

B.†

. . . The artillery of the press has been leveled against us, charged with whatsoever licentiousness could devise or dare. These abuses of an institution so important to freedom and science are deeply to be regretted, inasmuch as they tend to lessen its usefulness and to sap its safety. They might, indeed, have been corrected by the wholesome punishments reserved and provided by the laws of the several States against falsehood and defamation, but . . . the offenders have . . . been left to find their punishment in the public indignation.

Nor was it uninteresting to the world that an experiment should be fairly and fully made, whether freedom of discussion, unaided by power, is not sufficient for the

* Letter written in 1803. Published in S. K. Padover, *Jefferson* (1942), p. 330.
† Second Inaugural Address, March 4, 1805. Published in J. D. Richardson, ed., *A Compilation of the Messages and Papers of the Presidents,* I (1899), p. 381.

propagation and protection of truth. . . . The experiment has been tried; you have witnessed the scene; our fellow-citizens looked on, cool and collected . . . ; they gathered around their public functionaries, and . . . they pronounced their verdict. . . . The public judgment will correct false reasonings and opinions on a full hearing of all parties; and no other definite line can be drawn between the inestimable liberty of the press and its demoralizing licentiousness. If there be still improprieties which this rule would not restrain, its supplement must be sought in the censorship of public opinion.

— Reading No. 29 —

THE LOUISIANA PURCHASE*

The acquisition of New Orleans would of itself have been a great thing, as it would have ensured to our western brethren the means of exporting their produce: but that of Louisiana is inappreciable, because, giving us the sole dominion of the Mississippi, it excludes those bickerings with foreign powers, which we know of a certainty would have put us at war with France immediately; and it secures to us the course of a peaceable nation.

. . . But there is a difficulty in this acquisition which presents a handle to the malcontents among us, though they have not yet discovered it. Our confederation is certainly confined to the limits established by the revolution. The general government has no powers but such as the Constitution has given it; and it has not given it a power of holding foreign territory, & still less of incorporating it into the Union. An amendment of the Constitution seems necessary for this. In the meantime we must ratify & pay our money, as we have treated, for a thing beyond the Constitution, and rely on the nation to sanction an act done for its great good, without its previous authority.

* Letter to John Dickinson, August 9, 1803. Published in P. L. Ford, ed., *The Writings of Thomas Jefferson*, VIII (1897), pp. 261-262.

— Reading No. 30 —

JEFFERSON'S VIEW OF PUBLIC DEBT

A.*

I consider the fortunes of our republic as depending, in an eminent degree, on the extinguishment of the public debt before we engage in any war: because, that done, we shall have revenue enough to improve our country in peace and defend it in war, without recurring either to new taxes or loans. But if the debt should once more be swelled to a formidable size, its entire discharge will be despaired of, and we shall be committed to the English career of debt, corruption and rottenness, closing with revolution. The discharge of the debt, therefore, is vital to the destinies of our government. . . .

B.†

If we run into such debts, as that we must be taxed in our meat and in our drink, in our necessaries and our comforts, in our labors and our amusements, for our callings and our creeds, as the people of England are, our people, like them, must come to labor sixteen hours in the twenty-four, give the earnings of fifteen of these to the government for their debts and daily expenses; and the sixteenth being insufficient to afford us bread, we must live, as they now do, on oatmeal and potatoes; have no

---

* Letter to Secretary of the Treasury Albert Gallatin, October 11, 1809. Published in P. L. Ford, ed., *The Writings of Thomas Jefferson*, IX (1898), p. 264.

† Letter to Samuel Kercheval, July 12, 1816. Published in P. L. Ford, ed., *The Writings of Thomas Jefferson*, X (1899), pp. 41-42.

time to think, no means of calling the mismanagers to account; but be glad to obtain subsistence by hiring ourselves to rivet their chains on the necks of our fellow-sufferers.

— Reading No. 31 —

A THIRD TERM

A.

Opposition*

My opinion originally was that the President of the U.S. should have been elected for 7 years, & forever ineligible afterwards. I have since become sensible that 7 years is too long to be irremovable, and that there should be a peaceable way of withdrawing a man in midway who is doing wrong. The service for 8 years with a power to remove at the end of the first four, comes nearly to my principle as corrected by experience. And it is in adherence to that that I determined to withdraw at the end of my second term. The danger is that the indulgence & attachments of the people will keep a man in the chair after he becomes a dotard, that reelection through life shall become habitual, & election for life follow that. General Washington set the example of voluntary retirement after 8 years. I shall follow it, and a few more precedents will oppose the obstacle of habit to anyone after a while who shall endeavor to extend his term. Perhaps it may beget a disposition to establish it by an amendment to the Constitution.

B.

Views†

Jefferson was in Paris when the Constitution was made in Philadelphia. He received a copy of it early in Novem-

---

* Letter to John Taylor, January 6, 1805. Published in P. L. Ford, ed., *The Writings of Thomas Jefferson,* VIII (1897), p. 339.
† *Autobiography* (1821). Published in S. K. Padover, ed., *The Complete Jefferson* (1943), pp. 1171-1173.

ber 1787 and read it with great satisfaction. One of the articles of which he was critical, however, dealt with the Presidential term of office. In this selection from his Autobiography *one finds his final views on the subject.*

✓ ✓ ✓

. . . The re-eligibility of the President for life, I quite disapproved. . . . My fears of that feature were founded on the importance of the office, on the fierce contentions it might excite among ourselves, if continuable for life, and the dangers of interference, either with money or arms, by foreign nations, to whom the choice of an American President might become interesting. Examples of this abounded in history; in the case of the Roman Emperors, for instance; of the Popes . . . ; of the German Emperors; the Kings of Poland, and the Deys of Barbary. I had observed, too, in the feudal history, and in the recent instance . . . of the Stadtholder of Holland, how easily offices, or tenures for life, slide into inheritances. My wish, therefore, was, that the President should be elected for seven years, and be ineligible afterwards. This term I thought sufficient to enable him, with the concurrence of the Legislature, to carry through and establish any system of improvement he should propose for the general good.

But the practice adopted, I think, is better, allowing his continuance for eight years, with a liability to be dropped at half way of the term, making that a period of probation. . . . The example of four Presidents voluntarily retiring at the end of their eighth year, and the progress of public opinion, that the principle is salutary, have given it in practice the force of precedent and usage; insomuch, that, should a President consent to be a candidate for a third election, I trust he would be rejected, on this demonstration of ambitious views.

— Reading No. 32 —

GOVERNMENT AND THE PEOPLE*

At the formation of our government, many had formed their political opinions on European writings and practices. . . . The doctrines of Europe were, that men . . . cannot be restrained within the limits of order and justice, but by forces physical and moral, wielded over them by authorities independent of their will. Hence their organization of kings, hereditary nobles, and priests. Still further to constrain the brute force of the people, they deem it necessary to keep them down by hard labor, poverty and ignorance. . . .

[The Federalist party] endeavored to draw the cords of power as tight as they could . . . , to lessen the dependence of the general functionaries on their constituents. . . . Ours, on the contrary, was to maintain the will of the majority . . . of the people. . . . We believed . . . that man was a rational animal, endowed by nature with rights, and with an innate sense of justice; and that he could be restrained from wrong and protected in right, by moderate powers, confided to persons of his own choice. . . . We believed that the complicated organization of kings, nobles, and priests, was not the wisest nor best to effect the happiness of associated man; that wisdom and virtue were not hereditary. . . .

We believed that men, enjoying in ease and security the full fruits of their own industry, enlisted by all their interests on the side of law and order, habituated to think for themselves, and to follow their reason as their guide,

* Letter to William Johnson, June 12, 1823. Published in P. L. Ford, ed., *The Writings of Thomas Jefferson,* X (1899), pp. 226-227 n.

would be more easily and safely governed, than with minds nourished in error, and vitiated and debased, as in Europe, by ignorance, indigence and oppression. The cherishment of the people then was our principle, the fear and distrust of them, that of the other [*Federalist*] party.

— Reading No. 33 —

THE PEOPLE TO EXERCISE
ALL POSSIBLE POWER*

. . . I have read with great pleasure the paper you enclosed me on that subject [*political partisanship*]. . . . In reading it with great satisfaction, there was but a single passage where I wished a little more development of a very sound and catholic idea; a single intercalation to rest it solidly on true bottom. It is . . . where you make a statement of genuine republican maxims; saying, 'that the people ought to possess as much political power as can possibly exist with the order and security of society.' Instead of this, I would say, 'that the people, being the only safe depository of power, should exercise in person every function which their qualifications enable them to exercise, consistently with the order and security of society; that we now find them equal to the election of those who shall be invested with their executive and legislative powers, and to act themselves in the judiciary, as judges in questions of fact; that the range of their powers ought to be enlarged, &.' This gives both the reason and exemplification of the maxim you express, 'that they ought to possess as much political power, &.'

* Letter to Dr. Walter Jones, January 2, 1814. Published in P. L. Ford, ed., *The Writings of Thomas Jefferson,* IX (1898), p. 447.

— Reading No. 34 —

HUMAN NATURE AND
GOVERNMENT*

I have been amusing myself latterly with reading the voluminous letters of Cicero. They certainly breathe the purest effusions of an exalted patriot, while the parricide Caesar is lost in odious contrast. When the enthusiasm, however, kindled by Cicero's pen and principles, subsides into cool reflection, I ask myself, what was that government which the virtues of Cicero were so zealous to restore, and the ambition of Caesar to subvert? And if Caesar had been as virtuous as he was daring and sagacious, what could he, even in the plenitude of his usurped power, have done to lead his fellow citizens into good government? I do not say to *restore it*, because they never had it, from the rape of the Sabines to the ravages of the Caesars. If their people indeed had been, like ourselves, enlightened, peaceable, and really free, the answer would be obvious. . . . But steeped in corruption, vice and venality, as the whole nation was (and nobody had done more than Caesar to corrupt it), what could even Cicero, Cato, Brutus have done, had it been referred to them to establish a good government for their country? They had no ideas of government themselves, but of their degenerate Senate, nor the people of liberty, but of the factious opposition of their Tribunes. . . . No government can continue good, but under the control of the people; and their people were so demoralized and depraved, aas to be incapable of exercising a wholesome control. Their refor-

* Letter to John Adams, December 10, 1819. Published in P. L. Ford, ed., *The Writings of Thomas Jefferson*, X (1899), pp. 152-153.

mation then was to be taken up *ab incunabulis*. Their minds were to be informed by education what is right and what wrong; to be encouraged in habits of virtue, and deterred from those of vice by the dread of punishments, proportioned indeed, but irremissible; in all cases, to follow truth as the only safe guide, and to eschew error, which bewilders us in one false consequence after another, in endless succession. These are the inculcations necessary to render the people a sure basis for the structure of order and good government. But this would have been an operation of a generation or two, at least. . . .

— Reading No. 35 —

MORAL PRINCIPLES
OF GOVERNMENT*

. . . Distinguishing between the structure of the government and the moral principles on which you prescribe its administration, with the latter we concur cordially, with the former we should not. We of the United States, you know, are constitutionally and conscientiously democrats. We consider society as one of the natural wants with which man has been created; that he has been endowed with faculties and qualities to effect its satisfaction by concurrence of others having the same want. . . . I acknowledge myself strong in affection of our own form [*of government*], yet both of us act and think from the same motive, we both consider the people as our children, and love them with parental affection. But you love them as infants whom you are afraid to trust without nurses; and I as adults whom I freely leave to self-government. . . .

But when we come to the moral principles on which the government is to be administered, we come to what is proper for all conditions of society. . . . I believe with you that morality, compassion, generosity, are innate elements of the human constitution; that there exists a right independent of force; that a right to property is founded in our natural wants, in the means with which we are endowed to satisfy these wants, and the right to what we acquire by those means without violating the similar

* Letter to P. S. Dupont de Nemours, April 24, 1816. Published in P. L. Ford, ed., *The Writings of Thomas Jefferson*, X (1899), pp. 22-24; also in S. K. Padover, ed., *A Jefferson Profile* (1956), pp. 271-274.

rights of other sensible beings; that no one has a right to obstruct another, exercising his faculties innocently for the relief of sensibilities made a part of his nature; that justice is the fundamental law of society; that the majority, oppressing an individual, is guilty of a crime, abuses its strength, and by acting on the law of the strongest breaks up the foundations of society; that action by the citizens in person, in affairs within their reach and competence, and in all others by representatives, chosen immediately, and removable by themselves, constitutes the essence of a republic; that all governments are more or less republican in proportion as this principle enters more or less into their composition; and that a government by representation is capable of extension over a greater surface of country than one of any other form.

THE MORAL INSTINCT*

Some have made the *love of God* the foundation of morality. This, too, is but a branch of our moral duties, which are generally divided into duties to God and duties to man. If we did a good act merely from the love of God and a belief that it is pleasing to Him, whence arises the morality of the atheist? . . .

Self-interest, or rather self-love, or *egoism,* has been more plausibly substituted as the basis of morality. But I consider our relations with others as constituting the boundaries of morality. . . . To ourselves, in strict language, we can owe no duties, obligation requiring also two parties. Self-love, therefore, is no part of morality. Indeed, it is exactly its counterpoint. . . .

Egoism, in a broader sense, has been . . . presented as the source of moral action. It has been said that we feed the hungry, clothe the naked, bind up the wounds of the man beaten by thieves . . . , because we receive ourselves pleasure from these acts. So Helvétius [*defines*] . . . 'interest' to mean . . . whatever may procure us pleasure or withdraw us from pain. . . . This indeed is true. But it is one step short of the ultimate question.

These good acts give us pleasure, but how happens it that they give us pleasure? Because nature hath implanted in our breasts a love of others, a sense of duty to them, a moral instinct, in short, which prompts us irresistibly to feel and to succor their distress. . . . The Creator would indeed have been a bungling artist, had he intended man for a social animal, without planting in him social dispositions. . . .

* Letter to Thomas Law, June 13, 1814. Published in S. K. Padover, ed., *A Jefferson Profile* (1956), pp. 213-234.

Some have argued against the existence of a moral sense, by saying that if nature had given us such a sense, . . . then nature would also have designated, by some particular ear-marks, the two sets of actions which are, in themselves, the one virtuous and the other vicious. Whereas, we find, in fact, that the same actions are deemed virtuous in one country and vicious in another. The answer is that nature has constituted *utility* to man the standard . . . of virtue. . . .

I sincerely, then, believe with you in the general existence of a moral instinct. I think it the brightest gem with which the human character is studded, and the want of it as more degrading than the most hideous of the bodily deformities.

— Reading No. 37 —

THE PEOPLE'S ABILITY FOR SELF-GOVERNMENT*

We think in America that it is necessary to introduce the people into every department of government as far as they are capable of exercising it; and that this is the only way to ensure a long continued & honest administration of its powers. 1. They are not qualified to exercise themselves the Executive department; but they are qualified to name the person who shall exercise it. . . . 2. They are not qualified to legislate. With us, therefore, they only choose the legislators. They are not qualified to *judge* questions of *law;*† but they are very capable of judging questions of *fact*. In the form of juries, therefore, they determine all matters of fact, leaving to the permanent judges to decide the law resulting from those facts. . . . Were I called upon to decide whether the people had best be omitted in the Legislative or Judiciary department, I would say it is better to leave them out of the Legislature. The execution of the laws is more important than the making them. However, it is best to have the people in all the three departments where that is possible.

* To the Abbé François Arnaud, July 19, 1789. Published in P. L. Ford, ed., *The Writings of Thomas Jefferson*, V (1895), pp. 103-104.
† Italics in the original.

— Reading No. 39 —

OPPOSITION TO CENSORSHIP*

I am really mortified to be told that, in the United States of America, a fact like this† can become a subject of inquiry, and of criminal inquiry too, as an offence against religion; that a question about the sale of a book can be carried before the civil magistrate. Is this then our freedom of religion? And are we to have a censor whose imprimatur shall say what books may be sold, and what we may buy? And who is thus to dogmatize religious opinions for our citizens? Whose foot is to be the measure to which ours are all to be cut or stretched? Is a priest to be our inquisitor, or shall a layman, simple as ourselves, set up his reason as the rule for what we are to read, and what we must believe? It is an insult to our citizens to question whether they are rational beings or not, and blasphemy against religion to suppose it cannot stand the test of truth and reason. If M. de Becourt's book be false in its facts, disprove them; if false in its reasoning, refute it. But, for God's sake, let us freely hear both sides, if we choose.

* Letter to Dufief, April 19, 1814. Published in S. K. Padover, ed., *The Complete Jefferson* (1943), p. 889.
† The sale of a French book by de Becourt, *Sur la Création du Monde, un Système d'Organisation Primitif.*

— Reading No. 40 —

NATURAL RIGHT OF
ASSOCIATION*

A right of free correspondence between citizen & citizen, on their joint interest, whether public or private, & under whatsoever laws these interests arise (to wit, of the State, of Congress, of France, Spain, or Turkey), is a natural right; it is not the gift of any municipal law, either of England, or of Virginia, or of Congress; but in common with all our other natural rights, is one of the objects for the protection of which society is formed, & municipal laws established.

* Letter to James Monroe, September 7, 1797. Published in P. L. Ford, ed., *The Writings of Thomas Jefferson,* VII (1896), p. 172.

NATURAL RIGHT TO
SELF-GOVERNMENT*

Every man, and every body of men on earth, possesses the right of self-government. They receive it with their being from the hand of nature. Individuals exercise it by their single will; collections of men by that of their majority; for the law of the majority is the natural law of every society of men. When a certain description of men are to transact together a particular business, the times and places of their meeting and separating, depend on their own will; they make a part of the natural right of self-government. This, like all other natural rights, may be abridged or modified in its exercise by their own consent, or by the law of those who depute them, if they meet in the right of others; but as far as it is not abridged or modified, they retain it as a natural right, and may exercise them in what form they please. . . .

* Opinion on Residence Bill, July 15, 1790. Published in P. L. Ford, ed., *The Writings of Thomas Jefferson*, V (1895), pp. 205-206.

— Reading No. 42 —

DEFINITION OF A REPUBLIC*

. . . Indeed, it must be acknowledged, that the term *republic* is of very vague application in every language. Witness the self-styled republics of Holland, Switzerland, Genoa, Venice, Poland. Were I to assign to this term a precise and definite idea, I would say, purely and simply, it means a government by its citizens in mass, acting directly and personally, according to rules established by the majority; and that every other government is more or less republican, in proportion as it has in its composition more or less of this ingredient of the direct action of the citizens. Such a government is evidently restrained to very narrow limits of space and population. I doubt if it would be practicable beyond the extent of a New England township. The first shade from this pure element, which, like that of pure vital air, cannot sustain life of itself, would be where the powers of the government, being divided, should be exercised each by representatives chosen either *pro hac vice,* or for such short terms as should render secure the duty of expressing the will of their constituents. This I should consider as the nearest approach to a pure republic, which is practicable on a large scale of country or population. . . . Other shades of republicanism may be found in other forms of government, where the executive, judiciary and legislative functions, and the different branches of the latter, are chosen by the people more or less directly, for longer terms of years or for life, or made hereditary; or where there are

* Letter to John Taylor, May 28, 1816. Published in P. L. Ford, ed., *The Writings of Thomas Jefferson,* X (1899), pp. 28-31; also in S. K. Padover, ed., *A Jefferson Profile* (1956), pp. 277-281.

mixtures of authorities, some dependent on, and others independent of the people. The further the departure from direct and constant control by the citizens, the less has the government of the ingredient of republicanism; evidently none where the authorities are hereditary, as in France, Venice, etc., or self-chosen, as in Holland; and little, where for life. . . .

The purest republican feature in the government of our own State [*Virginia*], is the House of Representatives. The Senate is equally so the first year, less the second, and so on. The Executive still less, because not chosen by the people directly. The Judiciary seriously anti-republican, because for life. . . .

In the General Government, the House of Representatives is mainly republican; the Senate scarcely so at all, as not elected by the people directly, and so long secured even against those who do elect them; the Executive more republican than the Senate, from its shorter term . . . ; the Judiciary independent of the nation. . . .

On this view of . . . the term *republic*, instead of saying, as has been said, 'that it may mean anything or nothing,' we may say with truth and meaning, that governments are more or less republican as they have more or less of the element of popular election and control in their composition; and believing, as I do, that the mass of the citizens is the safest depository of their own rights, and especially, that the evils flowing from the duperies of the people, are less injurious than those from the egoism of their agents, I am a friend to that composition of government which has in it the most of this ingredient. . . .

THE CONSTITUTION—A
SAFEGUARD AGAINST ABUSE*

The observations are but too just which are made in your friendly address, on the origin and progress of those abuses of public confidence and power which have so often terminated in a suppression of the rights of the people and the mere aggrandizement and emolument of their oppressors. Taught by these truths, and aware of the tendency of power to degenerate into abuse, the worthies of our own country have secured its independence by the establishment of a constitution and form of government for our nation, calculated to prevent as well as to correct abuse.

* To Washington, D.C. Tammany Society, March 2, 1809.
  Published in S. K. Padover, ed., *The Complete Jefferson*
  (1943), pp. 551-552.

— Reading No. 44 —

CONSTITUTIONS MUST BE SUBJECT TO CHANGE*

Some men look at constitutions with sanctimonious reverence, and deem them like the arc of the covenant, too sacred to be touched. They ascribe to them of the preceding age a wisdom more than human, and suppose what they did to be beyond amendment. I knew that age well. . . . It was very like the present, but without the experience of the present; and forty years of experience in government is worth a century of book-reading. . . .

I am certainly not an advocate for frequent and untried changes in laws and constitutions. I think that moderate imperfections had better be borne with. . . . But I know also that laws and institutions must go hand in hand with the progress of the human mind. . . . Institutions must . . . keep pace with the times. We might as well require a man to wear still the coat which fitted him when a boy, as civilized society to remain ever under the regimen of their barbarous ancestors. . . .

Let us . . . avail ourselves of our reason and experience, to correct the crude essays of our first and unexperienced, although wise, virtuous, and well-meaning councils. And . . . let us provide in our constitution for its revision at stated periods.

* Letter to Samuel Kercheval, July 12, 1816. Published in P. L. Ford, ed., *The Writings of Thomas Jefferson*, X (1899), pp. 42-44; also in S. K. Padover, ed., *A Jefferson Profile* (1956), pp. 281-283.

— Reading No. 45 —

NATURAL RIGHTS*

Our legislators are not sufficiently apprized of the rightful limits of their power; that their true office is to declare and enforce only our natural rights and duties, and to take none of them from us. No man has a natural right to commit aggression on the equal rights of another; and this is all from which the laws ought to restrain him; every man is under the natural duty of contributing to the necessities of the society; and this is all the laws should enforce on him; and, no man having a natural right to be the judge between himself and another, it is his natural duty to submit to the umpirage of an impartial third. When the laws have declared and enforced all this, they have fulfilled their functions, and the idea is quite unfounded, that on entering into society we give up any natural right. . . .

* Letter to Francis W. Gilmer, June 7, 1816. Published in P. L. Ford, ed., *The Writings of Thomas Jefferson*, X (1899), p. 32.

CRITICISM OF JUDICIAL REVIEW*

In denying the right they [*Supreme Court judges*] usurp of exclusively explaining the constitution, I go further than you do, if I understand rightly your quotation from the Federalist, of an opinion that 'the judiciary is the last resort in relation *to the other departments* of the government, but not in relation to the rights of the parties to the compact under which the judiciary is derived.' If this opinion be sound, then indeed is our constitution a complete *felo de se*. For intending to establish three departments, co-ordinate and independent, that they might check and balance one another, it has given, according to this opinion, to one of them alone, the right to prescribe rules for the government of the others, and to that one too, which is unelected by, and independent of the nation. For experience has already shown that the impeachment it has provided is not even a scare-crow. . . . The constitution, on this hypothesis, is a mere thing of wax in the hands of the judiciary, which they may twist and shape into any form they please. It should be remembered as an axiom of eternal truth in politics, that whatever power in any government is independent, is absolute also; in theory only, at first, while the spirit of the people is up, but in practice, as fast as that relaxes. Independence can be trusted nowhere but with the people in mass. They are inherently independent of all but moral law. My construction of the constitution is very different from that you quote. It is that each department is truly independent of

* Letter to Judge Spencer Roane, September 6, 1819. Published in P. L. Ford, ed., *The Writings of Thomas Jefferson*, X (1899), pp. 140-141.

the others, and has an equal right to decide for itself what is the meaning of the constitution in the cases submitted to its action; and especially, where it is to act ultimately and without appeal.

NATURAL ARISTOCRACY*

The passage you quote from Theognis [*a 6th-century-*
B.C. *Greek poet*], I think has an ethical rather than a political object. The whole piece is a moral exhortation, and
this passage particularly seems to be a reproof to man,
who while with his domestic animals he is curious to improve the race, by employing always the finest male, pays
no attention to the improvement of his own race, but
intermarries with the vicious, the ugly, or the old, for
considerations of wealth or ambition. . . . The selecting
of the best male for a harem of well chosen females also,
which Theognis seems to recommend from the example
of our sheep and asses, would doubtless improve the human, as it does the brute animal, and produce a race of
veritable *aristoi*. For experience proves, that the moral
and physical qualities of man, whether good or evil, are
transmissible in a certain degree. . . . But I suspect that
the equal rights of men will rise up against this privileged
Solomon and his harem, and oblige us to . . . content
ourselves with the accidental *aristoi* produced by the for-
tuitous concourse of breeders.

For I agree with you that there is a natural aristocracy
among men. The grounds of this are virtue and talents.
Formerly, bodily powers gave place among the *aristoi*.
But since the invention of gunpowder has armed the weak
as well as the strong with missile death, bodily strength,
like . . . other accomplishments, has become but an
auxiliary ground for distinction. There is also an artificial

* Letter to John Adams, October 28, 1813. Published in P. L.
Ford, ed., *The Writings of Thomas Jefferson,* IX (1898),
pp. 424-429; also in S. K. Padover, ed., *A Jefferson
Profile* (1956), pp. 216-223.

aristocracy, founded on wealth and birth, without either virtue or talents; for with these it would belong to the first class. The natural aristocracy I consider as the most precious gift of nature, for the instruction, the trusts, and government of society. And, indeed, it would have been inconsistent in creation to have formed man for the social state, and not to have provided virtue and wisdom enough to manage the concerns of the society. May we not even say, that that form of government is the best, which provides the most effectually for a pure selection of these natural *aristoi* into the offices of government? The artificial aristocracy is a mischievous ingredient in government, and provision should be made to prevent its ascendancy.

CRITICISM OF THE SOCIETY OF THE CINCINNATI

The Society of the Cincinnati was formed, in June 1783, by officers who had served in the Continental Army during the American Revolution. George Washington was its first president and General Henry Knox its first secretary. The Society, with its gilded Orders and hereditary male membership, was feared by republicans, foremost among them Jefferson, as leading to the development of a class of hereditary nobles on the one side and plebeians on the other.

✦   ✦   ✦

A.*

I have never heard a person in Europe, learned or unlearned, express his thoughts on this institution [*Cincinnati*], who did not consider it as dishonorable & destructive to our governments, and . . . as the germ whose development is one day to destroy the fabric we have reared. I did not apprehend this while I had American ideas only. But I confess that what I have seen in Europe has brought me over to that opinion; & that though the day may be at some distance, beyond the reach of our lives perhaps, yet it will certainly come, when a single fibre left of this institution will produce an hereditary aristocracy which will change the form of our governments from the best to the worst in the world.

* Letter to George Washington, Paris, November 14, 1786. Published in P. L. Ford, ed., *The Writings of Thomas Jefferson*, IV (1894), pp. 328-329.

B.*

The objections of those who are opposed to the institution [*Cincinnati*] shall be briefly sketched. . . . They urge that it is against the Confederation—against the letter of some of our constitutions; against the spirit of all of them—that the foundation on which all these are built is the natural equality of man, the denial of every preeminence but that annexed to legal office, & particularly the denial of a preeminence by birth; that however, in their present dispositions, citizens might decline accepting honorary instalments into the order, a time may come when a change of dispositions would render these flattering, when a well directed distribution of them might draw into the order all the men of talents, of office & wealth, and in this case would probably procure an ingraftment into the government . . . ; that experience has shown that the hereditary branches of modern governments are the patrons of privilege & prerogative, & not of the natural rights of the people whose oppressors they generally are. . . .

* Letter to George Washington, April 16, 1784. Published in P. L. Ford, ed., *The Writings of Thomas Jefferson,* III (1894), pp. 466-467.

— Reading No. 49 —

INTELLIGENCE OF NEGROES

A.*

Comparing them, by their faculties of memory, reason, and imagination, it appears to me that in memory they are equal to the whites; in reason much inferior . . . , and in imagination they are dull, tasteless, and anomalous. . . . Never yet could I find that a black had uttered a thought above the level of plain narration; never seen even an elementary trait of painting or sculpture. In music they are generally more gifted than the whites, with accurate ears for tune and time. . . . Whether they will be equal to the composition of a more extensive run of melody, or of complicated harmony, is yet to be proved. . . .

Whether further observation will or will not verify the conjecture, that nature has been less bountiful to them in the endowment of the head, I believe that in those of the heart she will be found to have done them justice. . . . We find among them numerous instances of the most rigid integrity, and . . . of benevolence, gratitude, and unshaken fidelity.

The opinion that they are inferior in the faculties of reason and imagination, must be hazarded with great diffidence. To justify a general conclusion, requires many [more] observations. . . .

* *Notes on Virginia* (1782), Query **XIV**.

B.*

I have received . . . your . . . volume on the 'Literature of Negroes.' † Be assured that no person living wishes more sincerely than I do, to see a complete refutation of the doubts I have myself entertained and expressed on the grade of understanding allotted to them by nature, and to find that in this respect they are on a par with ourselves. My doubts were the result of personal observation in the limited sphere of my own State, where the opportunities for the development of their genius were not favorable, and those of exercising it still less so. I expressed them therefore with great hesitation; but whatever be their degree of talent it is no measure of their rights. Because Sir Isaac Newton was superior to others in understanding, he was not therefore lord of the person or property of others. On this subject they are gaining daily in the opinions of nations, and hopeful advances are making towards their re-establishment on an equal footing with the other colors of the human family. I pray you therefore to accept my thanks for the many instances you have enabled me to observe of the respectable intelligence in that race of men, which cannot fail to have effect in hastening the day of their relief.

* Letter to Henri Gregoire, February 25, 1809. Published in P. L. Ford, ed., *The Writings of Thomas Jefferson*, IX (1898), pp. 246-247.

† Gregoire (1750-1831), a French revolutionist and bishop, was interested in the emancipation of Negroes; he introduced the motion in the Constituent Assembly that gave them equal rights with whites in the French colonies.

PLAN FOR THE SOLUTION OF SLAVERY: EMANCIPATION AND RESETTLEMENT*

There were many plans to solve the slavery question. The one given below was published by Jefferson in 1782. A third of a century later, in 1815, he wrote that it was "still the one most sound in my judgment."

To emancipate all slaves born after the passing of the act. The bill reported by the revisers [*drafted by Jefferson between 1777 and 1779*] does not itself contain this proposition; but an amendment containing it was prepared, to be offered to the legislature whenever the bill should be taken up, . . . directing that they [*the slaves*] should continue with their parents to a certain age, then to be brought up, at the public expense, to tillage, arts, or sciences, according to their geniuses, till the females should be eighteen, and the males twenty-one years of age, when they should be colonized to such place as the circumstances of the time should render most proper, sending them out with arms, implements of household and of the handicraft arts, seeds, pairs of the useful domestic animals, &, to declare them a free and independent people, and extend to them our alliance and protection, till they have acquired strength; and to send vessels at the same time to other parts of the world for an equal number of white inhabitants; to induce them to migrate hither. . . . It will probably be asked, Why not

* *Notes on Virginia* (1782), Query XIV.

170

retain and incorporate the blacks into the State, and thus save the expense of supplying by importation of white settlers, the vacancies they will leave? Deep-rooted prejudices entertained by the whites; ten thousand recollections, by the blacks, of the injuries they have sustained; new provocations; the real distinctions which nature has made; and many other circumstances, will divide us into parties, and produce convulsions, which will probably never end but in the extermination of the one or the other race. To these objections, which are political, may be added others, which are physical and moral.

— Reading No. 51 —

JEFFERSON'S TREATMENT OF NEGROES*

In 1796, the Duke de la Rochefoucauld-Liancourt, in his tour of the United States, visited Monticello and left an interesting account of Jefferson's life at home, his habits, his personality, and his agricultural activities. The selection given below provides a rare glimpse of his relations with Negroes.

At present he is employed with activity and perseverance in the management of his farms and buildings; and he orders, directs, and pursues in the minutest detail every branch of business relative to them. I found him in the midst of the harvest, from which the scorching heat of the sun does not prevent his attendance. His Negroes are nourished, clothed, and treated as well as white servants could be. . . . Every article is made on his farm; his Negroes are cabinetmakers, carpenters, masons, bricklayers, smiths, &. The children he employs in a nail-manufactory, which yields already a considerable profit. The young and old Negresses spin for the clothing of the rest. He animates them by rewards and distinctions.

* Duke de la Rochefoucauld-Liancourt, *Travels Through the United States . . . , in the Years 1795, 1796, and 1797* (London, 1799), pp. 69 f.

— Reading No. 52 —

PROGRAM FOR CIVILIZING INDIANS*

. . . Supposing it will be satisfactory to you, and to those with whom you are placed,† to understand my personal dispositions and opinions in this particular [*the Indian problem*], I shall avail myself of this private letter to state them generally. I consider the business of hunting as already become insufficient to furnish clothing and subsistence to the Indians. The promotion of agriculture, therefore, and household manufacture, are essential in their preservation, and I am disposed to aid and encourage it liberally. This will enable them to live on much smaller portions of land, and indeed will render their vast forests useless but for the range of cattle; for which purpose, also, as they become better farmers, they will be found useless, and even disadvantageous. While they are learning to do better on less land, our increasing numbers will be calling for more land, and thus a coincidence of interests will be produced between those who have lands to spare, and want other necessaries, and those who have such necessaries to spare, and want lands. This commerce, then, will be for the good of both, and those who are friends to both ought to encourage it. You are in the station peculiarly charged with this interchange, and who have it peculiarly in your power to promote among the

* Letter to Benjamin Hawkins, February 18, 1803. Published in P. L. Ford, ed., *The Writings of Thomas Jefferson*, VIII (1897), pp. 213-215.

† Colonel Hawkins was the Federal Indian agent during Jefferson's Administration.

Indians a sense of the superior value of a little land, well cultivated, over a great deal, unimproved, and to encourage them to make this estimate truly. The wisdom of the animal which amputates & abandons to the hunter the parts for which he is pursued should be theirs, with this difference, that the former sacrifices what is useful, the latter what is not.

In truth, the ultimate point of rest & happiness for them is to let our settlements and theirs meet and blend together, to intermix, and become one people. Incorporating themselves with us as citizens of the U. S., this is what the natural progress of things will of course bring on, and it will be better to promote than to retard it. Surely it will be better for them to be identified with us, and preserved in the occupation of their lands, than to be exposed to the many casualties which may endanger them while a separate people. . . . This is the one [way] most for their happiness. . . . It is possible, perhaps probable, that this idea may be so novel as that it might shock the Indians, were it even hinted to them. Of course, you will keep it for your own reflection; but, convinced of its soundness, I feel it consistent with pure morality to lead them towards it, to familiarize them to the idea that it is for their interest to cede lands at times to the U. S.

— Reading No. 53 —

THE GREAT MORAL AND
RELIGIOUS LEADERS*

As you say of yourself, I too am an Epicurian. I consider the genuine (not the imputed) doctrines of Epicurus as containing everything rational in moral philosophy which Greece and Rome have left us. Epictetus, indeed, has given us what was good of the Stoics. . . . Their great crime was in their calumnies of Epicurus and misrepresentation of his doctrines; in which we lament to see the candid character of Cicero engaging as an accomplice. . . . His prototype Plato, eloquent as himself, dealing out mysticisms incomprehensible to the human mind, has been deified by certain sects usurping the name of Christians; because, in his foggy conceptions, they found a basis of impenetrable darkness whereon to rear fabrications as delirious, of their own invention. These they fathered blasphemously on him whom they claimed as their founder [*Jesus*], but who would disclaim them with the indignation which their caricatures of his religion so justly excite.

Of Socrates we have nothing genuine but in the Memorabilia of Xenophon; for Plato makes him one of his Collocutors merely to cover his own whimsies under the mantle of his own name; a liberty of which we are told Socrates himself complained. Seneca is indeed a fine moralist, disfiguring his work at times with some Stoicisms. . . .

* Letter to William Short, October 31, 1819. Published in
   P. L. Ford, ed., *The Writings of Thomas Jefferson*, X
   (1899), pp. 143-145.

But the greatest of all the reformers of the depraved religion of his own country was Jesus of Nazareth. Abstracting what is really his from the rubbish in which it is buried, easily distinguished by its lustre from the dross of his biographers, and as separable from that as the diamond from the dunghill, we have the outlines of a system of the most sublime morality which has ever fallen from the lips of man; outlines which it is lamentable he did not live to fill up. Epictetus and Epicurus give laws for governing ourselves, Jesus a supplement of the duties and charities we owe to others. . . . I have sometimes thought of translating Epictetus . . . by adding the genuine doctrines of Epicurus . . . and an abstract from the Evangelists of whatever has the stamp of the eloquence and fine imagination of Jesus. . . .

I take the liberty of observing that you are not a true disciple of our master Epicurus, in indulging in indolence. . . . One of his canons, you know, was that 'the indulgence which prevents a greater pleasure, or produces a greater pain, is to be avoided.' . . . Fortitude, you know, is one of his [*Epicurus'*] four cardinal virtues. That teaches us to meet and surmount difficulties; not to fly from them like cowards; and to fly, too, in vain, for they will meet and arrest us at every turn of our road. . . .

— Reading No. 54 —

RELIGION

A.

Opposition to Uniformity*

Suppose the state should take into [*its*] head that there should be an uniformity of countenance. Men would be obliged to put an artificial bump or swelling here, a patch there, &. But this would be merely hypocritical. Or if the alternative was given of wearing a mask, 99/100ths must immediately mask. Would this add to the beauty of nature? Why otherwise in opinions? In the Middle Ages of Christianity opposition to the state opinions was hushed. The consequence was Christianity became loaded with all the Romish follies. Nothing but free argument, raillery, & even ridicule will preserve the purity of religion.

B.

The Rights of Conscience †

Our rulers can have authority over such natural rights, only as we have submitted to them. The rights of conscience we never submitted, we could not submit. We

* "Notes on Religion," October 1776. Published in J. P. Boyd, ed., *The Papers of Thomas Jefferson*, I (1950), pp. 548-549; also in S. K. Padover, ed., *The Complete Jefferson* (1943), p. 939. These were literally "notes," jotted down by Jefferson in abbreviated form; in the text above the words are spelled out in full ("opinions" for "opn," etc.).

† *Notes on Virginia* (1782), Query XVII. Published in P. L. Ford, ed., *The Writings of Thomas Jefferson,* III (1894), pp. 262-266; also in S. K. Padover, ed., *The Complete Jefferson* (1943), pp. 674-676.

are answerable for them to our God. The legitimate powers of government extend to such acts only as are injurious to others. But it does me no injury for my neighbor to say there are twenty gods, or no God. It neither picks my pocket nor breaks my leg. If it be said his testimony in a court of justice cannot be relied on, reject it then, and be the stigma on him. Constraint may make him worse by making him a hypocrite, but it will never make him a truer man. It may fix him obstinately in his errors, but will not cure him.

Reason and free inquiry are the only effectual agents against error. Give a loose to them, they will support the true religion by bringing every false one to their tribunal, to the test of their investigation. Had not the Roman government permitted free inquiry, Christianity could never have been introduced. Had not free inquiry been indulged, at the era of the Reformation, the corruptions of Christianity could not have been purged away. If it be restrained now, the present corruptions will be protected, and new ones encouraged.

Was [*i.e., were*] the government to prescribe to us our medicine and diet, our bodies would be in such keeping as our souls are now. Thus in France the emetic was once forbidden as a medicine, and the potato as an article of food. Government is just as fallible, too, when it fixes systems in physics. Galileo was sent to the Inquisition for affirming that the earth was a sphere; the government had declared it to be as flat as a trencher, and Galileo was obliged to abjure his error. This error, however, at length prevailed, the earth became a globe, and Descartes declared it was whirled round its axis by a vortex. The government in which he lived was wise enough to see that this was no question of civil jurisdiction, or we should all have been involved by authority in vortices. In fact, the vortices have been exploded, and the Newtonian principle of gravitation is now more firmly established, on the basis of reason, than it would be were the government to step in and make it an article of faith. Reason and experiment have been indulged, and error has fled before them.

It is error alone which needs the support of government. Truth can stand by itself. Subject opinion to coercion;

whom will you make your inquisitors? Fallible men; men governed by bad passions, by private as well as public reasons. And why subject it to coercion? To produce uniformity. But is uniformity desirable? No more than of face and stature. Introduce the bed of Procrustes then, and as there is danger that the large men may beat the small, make us all of a size, by lopping the former and stretching the latter.

Difference of opinion is advantageous in religion. The several sects perform the office of a *censor morum* over each other. Is uniformity attainable? Millions of innocent men, women, and children, since the introduction of Christianity, have been burnt, tortured, fined, imprisoned; yet we have not advanced one inch towards uniformity. What has been the effect of coercion? To make one-half the world fools, and the other half hypocrites. To support roguery and error all over the earth.

Let us reflect that it is inhabited by a thousand millions of people. That these profess probably a thousand different systems of religion. That ours is but one of that thousand. That if there be but one right, and ours that one, we should wish to see the 999 wandering sects gathered into the fold of truth. But against such a majority we cannot effect this by force. Reason and persuasion are the only practicable instruments. To make way for these, free inquiry must be indulged; and how can we wish others to indulge it while we refuse it ourselves.

But every state, says an inquisitor, has established some religion. 'No two, say I, have established the same.' Is this a proof of the infallibility of establishments? Our sister states of Pennsylvania and New York, however, have long subsisted without any establishment at all. The experiment was new and doubtful when they made it. It has answered beyond conception. They flourish infinitely. Religion is well supported; of various kinds, indeed, but all good enough; all sufficient to preserve peace and order: or if a sect arises whose tenets would subvert morals, good sense has fair play, and reasons and laughs it out of doors, without suffering the state to be troubled by it. They do not hang more malefactors than we do. They are not more disturbed with religious dissensions. On the contrary, their harmony is unparalleled, and can

be described to nothing but their unbounded tolerance.
. . . They have made the happy discovery, that the way
to silence religious disputes, is to take no notice of them.

Let us, too, give this experiment fair play, and get rid,
while we may, of those tyrannical laws. It is true we are
as yet secured against them by the spirit of the times. I
doubt whether the people of this country would suffer an
execution for heresy, or a three years imprisonment for
not comprehending the mysteries of the trinity. But is the
spirit of the people an infallible, permanent reliance? Is
it government? . . . The spirit of the times may alter, will
alter. Our rulers will become corrupt, our people care-
less. A single zealot may commence persecutor, and better men be his victims. It can never be too often repeated, that the time for fixing every essential right on a
legal basis is while our rulers are honest, and ourselves
united.

FEDERAL GOVERNMENT CANNOT INTERMEDDLE IN RELIGIOUS AFFAIRS*

I consider the government of the U. S. as interdicted by the Constitution from intermeddling with religious institutions, their doctrines, discipline, or exercises. This results not only from the provision that no law shall be made respecting the establishment, or free exercise, of religion, but from that also which reserves to the states the powers not delegated to the U. S. Certainly no power to prescribe any religious exercise, or to assume authority in religious discipline, has been delegated to the general government. It must then rest with the states, as far as it can be in any human authority. . . .

I do not believe it is for the interest of religion to invite the civil magistrate to direct its exercises, its discipline, or its doctrines; nor of the religious societies that the general government should be invested with the power of effecting any uniformity of time or matter among them. Fasting & prayer are religious exercises. The enjoining them an act of discipline. Every religious society has a right to determine for itself the times for these exercises, & the objects proper for them, according to their own particular tenets; and this right can never be safer than in their own hands, where the Constitution has deposited it.

* Letter to the Rev. Samuel Miller, January 23, 1808. Published in P. L. Ford, ed., *The Writings of Thomas Jefferson,* IX (1898), pp. 174-175.

I am aware that the practice of my predecessors may be quoted. But I have ever believed that the example of State executives led to the assumption of that authority by the general government, without due examination, which would have discovered that what might be a right in a State government, was a violation of that right when assumed by another. Be this as it may, every one must act according to the dictates of his own reason, & mine tells me that civil powers alone have been given to the President of the U. S. and no authority to direct the religious exercises of his constituents.

— Reading No. 56 —

THE PRICELESS IMPORTANCE
OF EDUCATION*

I think by far the most important bill in our whole code is that for the diffusion of knowledge among the people. No other sure foundation can be devised, for the preservation of freedom and happiness. . . . Preach, my dear Sir, a crusade against ignorance; establish & improve the law for educating the common people. Let our countrymen know that the people alone can protect us against these evils [*monarchical and class rule*], and that the tax which will be paid for this purpose is not more than the thousandth part of what will be paid to kings, priests & nobles who will rise up among us if we leave the people in ignorance.

* Letter to George Wythe, Paris, August 13, 1786. Published in P. L. Ford, ed., *The Writings of Thomas Jefferson,* IV (1894), pp. 226-267.

THE USES OF HISTORY IN EDUCATION*

But of all the views of this law [*"A Bill for the More General Diffusion of Knowledge"*] none is more important, none more legitimate, than that of rendering the people the safe, as they are the ultimate, guardians of their own liberty. For this purpose the reading in the first stage, where *they* will receive their whole education, is proposed . . . to be chiefly historical. History, by apprising them of the past, will enable them to judge of the future; it will avail them of the experience of other times and other nations; it will qualify them as judges of the actions and designs of men; it will enable them to know ambition under every disguise it may assume; and knowing it, to defeat its views.

* *Notes on Virginia* (1782), Query XIV.

EDUCATION AND HAPPINESS*

. . . That every man shall be made virtuous, by any process whatever, is, indeed, no more to be expected than that every tree shall be made to bear fruit, and every plant nourishment. The brier and bramble can never become the vine and olive; but their asperities may be softened by culture, and their properties improved to usefulness in the order and economy of the world. And I do hope that, in the present spirit of extending to the great mass of mankind the blessings of instruction, I see a prospect of great advancement in the happiness of the human race; and that this may proceed to an indefinite, although not to an infinite degree.

* Letter to Cornelius C. Blatchly, October 21, 1822. Published in A. A. Lipscomb and A. E. Bergh, eds., *The Writings of Thomas Jefferson*, XV (1903), pp. 399-400.

BIBLIOGRAPHY

Collected Works

Major Collections:

Boyd, J. P., and others, *The Papers of Thomas Jefferson* (1950), and continuing, to a total of about 55 vols.

Ford, P. L., *The Writings of Thomas Jefferson*, 10 vols. (1892-1899)

Lipscomb, A. A., and Bergh, A. E., *The Writings of Thomas Jefferson*, 20 vols. (1903)

Randolph, T. J., *Memoir, Correspondence and Miscellanies, from the Papers of Thomas Jefferson*, 4 vols. (1829)

Smaller Collections:

Cappon, L. J., *The Adams-Jefferson Letters*, 2 vols. (1959)

Chinard, G., *The Commonplace Book of Thomas Jefferson* (1927)

Chinard, G., *The Correspondence of Jefferson and Du Pont de Nemours* (1931)

Chinard, G., *The Letters of Lafayette and Jefferson* (1929)

Ford, W. C., *Thomas Jefferson Correspondence. Printed from the Collection of . . . Bixby* (1916)

Malone, D., *Correspondence between Jefferson and . . . Du Pont* (1930)

Padover, S. K., *The Complete Jefferson* (1943); *A Jefferson Profile* (1956); *Thomas Jefferson on Democracy* (1946); *Thomas Jefferson and the National Capital* (1946)

Biographies

Bowers, C. G., *Jefferson and Hamilton* (1925); *Jefferson in Power* (1936); *The Young Jefferson* (1945)

Chinard, G., *Thomas Jefferson, The Apostle of Americanism* (1933)

Kimball, M., *Jefferson, The Road to Glory* (1943); *Jefferson, War and Peace* (1947); *Jefferson, The Scene of Europe* (1950)

Malone, D., *Jefferson the Virginian* (1948); *Jefferson and the Rights of Man* (1951); *Jefferson and the Ordeal of Liberty* (1963). This admirable multi-volume biography is still continuing.

Padover, S. K., *Jefferson* (1942)

Schachner, N., *Thomas Jefferson*, 2 vols. (1951)

Histories of the Period

Adams, H., *A History of the United States During the Administration of Thomas Jefferson*, 4 vols. (1889-1890)

Beard, C. A., *Economic Origins of Jeffersonian Democracy* (1915)

Bemis, S. F., *Thomas Jefferson,* in *American Secretaries of State,* Vol. II (1927)

Channing, E., *The Jeffersonian System* (1906)

Sears, L., *Jefferson and the Embargo* (1927)

White, L. D., *The Jeffersonians* (1951)

Special Studies

Berman, E. D., *Thomas Jefferson Among the Arts* (1947)

Conant, J. B., *Thomas Jefferson and the Development of American Education* (1962)

Eckardt, U. M. von, *The Pursuit of Happiness in the Democratic Creed* (1959)

Edwards, E. E., *Jefferson and Agriculture* (1943)

Honeywell, R. J., *The Educational Work of Thomas Jefferson* (1931)

Koch, A., *The Philosophy of Thomas Jefferson* (1943); *Jefferson and Madison: The Great Collaboration* (1950)

Martin, E., *Thomas Jefferson: Scientist* (1952)

Mott, F. L., *Jefferson and the Press* (1943)

Patterson, C. P., *The Constitutional Principles of Thomas Jefferson* (1953)

Peterson, M. D., *The Jefferson Image in the American Mind* (1960)

Wiltse, C. M., *The Jeffersonian Tradition in American Democracy* (1935)

INDEX

VAN NOSTRAND ANVIL BOOKS already published

478